Civilizational changes and the competitiveness of modern enterprises

by Marzena Grzesiak, Anita Richert-Kaźmierska

Published by
Baltic Sea Academy e.V.
Dr Max Hogefoster
Blankeneser Landstrasse, 22587 Hamburg, Germany

Editorial Correspondence: editor@baltic-sea-academy.eu;

Manufactured and published by BoD-Books on Demand, Norderstedt, Germany
© 2014 Baltic Sea Academy e.V. All rights reserved.

ISBN 9783732282449

.

Part-financed by the European Union (European Development Fund and European Neighbourhood and Partnership Instrument) within BSR QUICK IGA project. This publication does not necessarily reflect the opinion of the European Commision.

We are very grateful to the European Commision for the financial support and also to the Joint Technical Secretariat of the INTERREG IVB Programme for the support and advice.

Content

Foreword

The project "Innovative SMEs by Gender and Age (QUICK-IGA)" addresses the following objectives:

- levelling of equal opportunities for women south of the Baltic Sea with the ones of northern countries;
- strengthening the promotion of innovation in small and medium-sized enterprises by developing working cultures that explicitly improve the equal opportunities of women;
- supporting regional development in order to optimally develop human capital and competitiveness through gender and education policy.

On four levels the project focuses on the following activities:

1. Individuals: boosting motivation and work ability, thus increasing the rate of women participating in working life, through the training and education of consultants and the development of a manual;

2. Enterprises: fostering working conditions that meet women's needs and personnel development through the transfer of best practice, qualifications and coaching.

3. Organisations: competences and commitment of 45 chambers and 15 universities to supporting innovation and equal opportunities.

4. Policy: developing a strategy programme, five regional/national agreements and two action programmes to promote equal opportunities and innovation in SMEs.

The outputs and results of the project were published in the Baltic Sea Academy series for the following activities:

Data and principles

Two investigations were carried out for the countries and regions of the Baltic Sea region as the consistent basis for all further work:

a)   demographic and economic analysis in the BSR countries and regions;

b)   analysis of regional education and labour markets.

The results of these investigations were published in spring 2013 as part of the Baltic Sea Academy series under the title "Economic Perspectives, Qualification and Labour Market Integration of Women in the Baltic Sea Region".

Education

The results of the analysis have been incorporated into two new education products:

a) concept and curriculum for a train the trainer programme for the permanent implementation of training courses for consultants by universities and academies;

b) concept and curricula for a training and coaching programme for consultants to enhance their advisory competences on improving work structures in SMEs in order to increase the labour participation of women and older people, as well as innovation capacities.

Both training courses have been trialled multiple times in various locations and scientifically evaluated. The curricula, lecturer slides, execution instructions and evaluation results have been published in the form of a handbook.

Best practice

Analysis and preparation of 10 best practice cases on the promotion of labour market participation by women and older people, especially from Denmark, Sweden, Norway and Finland and transfer to the countries south of the Baltic Sea. The specific national conditions were investigated in order to allow implementation in the recipient countries.

The analysis of the conditions for the transfer of best practices and the 10 best practices have been published in the Baltic Sea Academy series of publications.

Regional/national cooperation's

Drafting and completion of memoranda of understanding on promoting innovative SMEs through women's entrepreneurship, and the increased employment of women and older people in Latvia, Lithuania, Belarus, North Poland and North Germany.

The memoranda containing the support activities to be implemented by the signatory institutions have been published in a manual.

Strategy programme

Strategic programme to promote innovation and the labour market participation of women and older people in SMEs as well as to increase the attractiveness of regional labour markets.

The strategy programme and two action plans (see below) were published as part of the Baltic Sea Academy series of publications.

Action plans

In order to involve 50 economic chambers and 16 universities in all the Baltic Sea countries in promoting the employment of women and older people in SMEs on a permanent basis, two action programmes have been developed and enacted:

a) action programme for 50 SME promoters (chambers + associations) in all BSR countries on promoting higher labour market participation by women and older people and, thus, increasing innovation capacities in SMEs;

b) action programme for 16 academies/universities from 9 Baltic Sea countries on the promotion and qualification of consultants to support the labour market participation of women and older people.

The action plans and appendix were published alongside the strategy programme (see above) in the Baltic Sea Academy series of publications.

International consultancy and transfer conferences

In order to achieve the highest possible and sustainable implementation of the target project results across all the Baltic Sea Countries, in 2013 and 2014 written transfer was supported by two consultancy and transfer conferences lasting several days with representatives from all the Baltic Sea countries. All the presentations and consultancy results developed were published in the Baltic Sea Academy series of publications in the following articles:

a) Corporate Social Responsibility and Women`s Entrepreneurship around the Mare Balticum.

b) Innovative SMEs by Gender and Age around the Mare Balticum.

Country-specific activities

During the project, it became clear that there was a need for more in-depth, further-reaching work in some countries to the south of the Baltic Sea. The following additional activities were also carried out to cover this:

Germany

Analysis of businesswomen in Germany, including a survey.

Poland

a) organisation and evaluation of a conference on "Development of the competitiveness of enterprises in the context of demographic challenges";

b) analysis and elaboration on the employment of women and older people and its promotion;

c) analysis of women's activities in SMEs in Poland and scenarios for possible future development.

Lithuania

Theoretical analytical study of political activities: Building the socially responsible employment policy in Baltic states

The results of these five additional activities were published in the Baltic Sea Academy series of publications.

Manual

Development and publication of a manual on promoting innovation through increasing the labour market participation of women and older people and the proportion of female entrepreneurs in SMEs.

This publication provides some of the relevant scientific background for the work described above.

"I can not predict, but I can lay the groundwork.
Because the future is something that is to be built."

Antoine de Saint-Exupery

Introduction

The times we live in are characterized by an amazing variation affecting all aspects of our lives: behaviours, norms and values — the organizations, their structures and cultures, as well as environment in which these transformations are taking place, are changing. Since the mid-twentieth century, the environment in which we operate is in fact described as turbulent, i.e. characterised by an unprecedented amount, rate, intensity and complexity of changes [Ansoff 1988].

Among the most important reasons determining the changes in recent decades, the literature lists the following phenomena [Bolesta-Kukułka 1993, p. 220-227; Koźmiński, Jamielniak 2011, p. 327]:

— globalization of the economy,
— development of technology, including information technology,
— individualization of consumer behaviours,
— changes in climate and environment in general,
— social changes, related mainly to demography and culture,
— changes in the global balance of political forces, including the creation of the international economic, political or military structures — new centres of power are created and new, transnational legal regulations are formulated.

In such a volatile environment the survival of an enterprise, and the more so its development and maintenance of high competitive position, seem to be extremely difficult. On the one hand, changes can create opportunities and provide the enterprises with chances for the development, on the other — restrict or even block the possibility of their functioning in the market. The role of an entrepreneur (the enterprise management) is therefore the observation of environment, forecasting of the impending changes and planning development based on the results of in-depth of macroeconomic and social etc. analyses.

In the monograph we are giving into the hands of readers, an attempt was made at classifying the civilization changes the modern entrepreneurs have to face in the fight for maintaining high competitiveness of their enterprises. Due to the scientific interests of authors, most attention was paid to the changes related to the progressive ageing of the population and the importance of innovation.

This book is a scientific publication — for the purpose of its drafting, a review of most recent scientific literature on enterprise competitiveness and innovation and the direction and pace of socio-economic changes, with a particular focus on demographic changes, was conducted. The practical value of the publication, on the other hand, should be emphasized due to: a review of existing national and international regulations in the field of enterprise activity, including their innovative activity, as well as examples of good practice of using the changes (mainly the demographic ones) to build the competitive advantage of enterprises.

The book is divided into six main parts. In the first part the authors present the direction and pace of current global civilization changes — particular attention was paid to globalization, technological development (mainly ICT) and demographic changes. Part two is entirely devoted to the issue of competitiveness. Among others, the factors and measures of competitiveness of modern enterprises, the level of competitiveness of enterprises in the European Union and the determinants of competitiveness of Polish enterprises are discussed. The third part contains an in-depth analysis of the concepts of innovation and innovativeness, as well as the classification of enterprise innovation metrics. It also discusses the European innovation policy and presents and evaluates the level of enterprise innovativeness in the Baltic Sea Region. The next part is devoted to the problems of an ageing population in Europe and the consequences of this process for enterprises. In the fifth part, the authors undertake a discussion on the possibilities of building the competitiveness of enterprises in the optimization of human resources which are traditionally marginalized in the labour market. The last part presents good practices of the economic activation of seniors and other disadvantaged groups. Examples of solutions based on the integration of individuals traditionally perceived as excluded from the labour market, used by enterprises (or organizations of other types) in the Baltic Sea Region are shown.

The book was written as a result of the authors' research work, conducted within the framework of the "Innovative SMEs by Gender and Age - QUICK-IGA" international project[1].

Marzena Grzesiak, Anita Richert-Kaźmierska

---

[1] The book was prepared as a part of the project *Quick IGA*, part-financed by European Union (European Regional Development Fund) in Baltic Sea Region Programme 2007–2013. Research paper financed from the funds for science 2012–2013 for co-financed international projects.

Chapter I The direction and pace of civilization changes

1.1. Globalisation as an economic and social phenomenon

The analysis of business processes requires taking into account a number of components which directly and indirectly affect their internal structure and pace, as well as the opportunities and conditions for further expansion. An important aspect is certainly the background of civilization: the current socio-economic order.

Civilization is "the developmental stage of a society in a particular historical period, conditioned by the level of its material culture, the degree of mastery of nature, the degree of development of productive forces, the total accumulated wealth, institutions, etc." [*Słownik wyrazów obcych* 1991, p. 164], in other words — the method of the structure of collective life [Piskozub 2000, p. 9-17]. The main attributes of modern post-industrial civilization[2] are: globalization, the knowledge society, advanced technologies and demographic changes.

Globalization is something relatively new and ambiguously defined. As Piasecki suggests, it is "a qualitatively completely new phenomenon that did not exist 50 or 100 years ago. (...) The difficulties in defining the exact term arise mainly from the fact that it is a very heterogeneous set of phenomena, processes and trends taking place in the modern world" [Piasecki 2003, p. 72-73]. In the literature, there are many definitions of globalization, suggesting different approaches to this phenomenon (see Table 1).

Table 1. Selected approaches to defining the concept of globalization

The proposed approach	Definitions	Author(s)
Process-oriented	Globalization as a complex of processes	[Barnet, Cavanagh 1994]
	The process of changes taking place simultaneously in many areas of social life: the economy, politics, military, culture	[Zaorska 2000]
Attribute-oriented	The internationalization of production, distribution and marketing of goods and services	[Harris 1993]
	Multidimensionality, complexity and multithreading, merging (integration), an international interdependence, relationship to the progress of science, technology and organization, the compression of time and space, the dialectical nature	[Zorska 1998]
	Irreversibility	[Barber 2000]
Relating to territo-	The process that is created by global phenomena	[Sundram, Black 1995]

---

[2] In the literature, the concept of post-industrial civilization is sometimes used interchangeably with the term "information civilization" or "civilization of knowledge".

rial ecoverage	or activities	
	The global system that is linked by international transactions and processes	[Michalak 1995]
	Moving decision-making to the regional or inter-national level	[Woods 2000]
	Action at a distance as the essence of the process of globalization	[Giddens 1997]

Source: own work.

In the broadest sense, globalization is "a process of deepening global linkages within all aspects of contemporary political, social, economic and cultural life" [Liberska 2002, p. 17]. As seen in the economic and political context, globalization means finding new areas and ways for expansion of capital, whereas in the context of civilization and culture, it can be understood as the emergence of a new global civilization and culture resulting from simultaneous confrontation and interpenetration of existing cultures and civilizations [Stacewicz 1998, p. 119].

While creating the ranking of the world's most globalized economies, the Ernst & Young and Economist Intelligence Unit experts take into account 20 indicators measuring the degree of international integration of business, grouped into five main categories: openness to trade, capital flows, exchange of technology and knowledge, labour mobility and cultural integration (see Table 2).

Table 2. The ranking of world's most globalized economies 2012 - Globalization Index

Place in the rank-ing	Country	Indica-tor value	Change since 2011	Change since 1995	Trade	Capital flows	La-bour	Tech-nology	Cul-ture
1.	HK	7.81	0.06	1.95	8.27	8.45	4.81	8.54	8.69
2.	SG	6.31	-0.02	1.01	8.67	6.04	4.80	5.56	6.31
3.	IE	5.63	0.06	1.20	6.32	6.04	5.90	3.68	6.36
4.	BE	5.49	0.11	1.17	6.39	6.64	5.50	4.27	4.29
5.	CH	5.30	0.04	1.49	6.32	6.64	6.15	4.33	5.06
6.	NL	5.19	0.02	0.92	6.24	6.59	5.19	4.49	4.21
7.	SE	4.96	0.01	0.97	6.27	5.29	4.82	4.07	4.12
8.	DK	4.94	0.01	0.92	5.88	5.33	4.68	4.26	4.12
9.	HU	4.76	0.07	1.02	6.63	4.15	5.03	3.32	3.92
10.	UK	4,74	0.03	0.63	5.89	4.81	4.83	3.94	4.06
11.	DE	4.72	0.03	0.87	6.47	4.58	4.36	3.92	4.00
12.	SK	4.66	0.09	1.53	5.29	4.16	4.76	3.74	4.22
13.	FI	4.62	0.03	0.71	6.73	4.90	4.42	3.96	3.67
14.	FR	4.58	0.04	0.57	5.41	4.55	4.77	3.97	4.08
15.	CA	4.56	0.00	0.73	5.06	4.79	4.36	3.90	4.60
16.	IL	4.55	0.01	0.64	5.76	4.36	4.41	3.32	4.69
17.	TW	4.55	0.02	0.88	5.68	4.24	4.56	4.03	3.87

18.	CZ	4.53	0.07	0.91	5.16	4.42	4.46	3.76	3.63
19.	AT	4.51	0.03	0.73	5.89	4.95	4.14	3.84	3.41
20.	ES	4.45	0.00	0.48	5.55	4.37	5.02	3.28	3.86
21.	NZ	4.44	0.05	0.68	5.49	4.48	4.24	3.81	4.05
22.	BG	4.37	0.04	1.25	6.31	4.05	4.80	2.91	3.58
23.	NO	4.36	0.01	0.85	5.33	4.46	4.51	4.12	3.11
24.	AU	4.34	0.04	0.57	5.30	4.59	4.39	3.49	3.77
25.	USA	4.33	0.02	0.58	5.32	4.57	4.16	3.62	3.79
26.	MY	4.28	0.07	0.38	5.21	4.18	3.50	3.89	3.13
27.	PL	4.23	0.06	1.27	5.80	4.01	4.53	3.17	3.68
28.	CL	4.22	0.04	0.50	5.61	5.07	4.19	2.61	3.38
29.	PT	4.21	0.01	0.14	4.93	4.02	5.50	3.11	3.42

Source: [*Indeks globalizacji gospodarek światowych* 2012].

The globalization index is a measure of the depth of the world's 60 largest economies' links with foreign countries. The first three positions in the ranking for 2012 were occupied by: Hong Kong, Ireland and Singapore. As in previous years, the group of countries with the highest index includes only few with population exceeding 10 million (in 2012 only two such countries were in the top ten of the ranking). The reason for this is that the index measures the degree of globalization in relative way, as the relationship of the international integration in terms of trade, investment, technology, labour and culture to the Gross Domestic Product.

In the 2012 ranking Poland was on the 27th place. The factor acting to the detriment of our country is the low level of investment in research and development. The indicators related to the openness to trade and capital flows, cultural integration and labour mobility appear good, on the other hand.

The deepening of globalization is accompanied by a number of socio-economic changes. They can be observed both in the macro perspective, relating to the economy and society as a whole, and in terms of microeconomy, i.e. individuals and companies.

The effect of globalization includes limiting the role of states in shaping the economic order. As Kaczmarczyk writes, "the Forbes Global 2000 ranking leaves no doubt who rules the world" [Kaczmarczyk 2013a]. The main players in the market are large multinational corporations whose revenues are greater than the budgets of many countries, including Germany — the strongest European economy as of now (see Table 3 and 4).

Table 3. The largest companies in the world in 2012 by Forbes

Position	Company	Country	Sales (U.S. $ bn)	Net profit (U.S. $ bn)	Market value

					(U.S. $ bn)
1.	Exxon Mobile	USA	433.5	41.1	407.4
2.	JP Morgan Chase	USA	110.8	19	170.1
3.	General Electric	USA	147.3	14.2	213.7
4.	Royal Dutch Shell	NL	470.2	30.9	227.6
5.	ICBC	CN	82.6	25.1	237.4

Source: http://www.forbes.pl/rankingi/najwieksze-firmy-swiata-2012,26185,1 (9.11.2013).

Table 4. The value of GDP in 2012: the weakest economies of the European Union

Country	GDP (USD billion)
MT	8,72
EE	21.85
CY	22.98
LV	28,32
LT	42,08
SI	45,28
BG	51,03

Source: World Bank.

The individual countries lose their significance (in all dimensions of their distinctiveness, self-reliance and self-governance), which embodies the concept of McLuhan's global village [McLuhan 1962]. A reality is created in which modern technologies allow for the blurring of the boundaries of time and space, and the unification of lifestyles, culture and consumption follows. As Robertson writes, "globalization is a set of processes that make the world socially uniform" [Robertson 1992]. The people, societies, cultures and civilizations that were previously isolated begin to communicate with each other regularly. As a result, new, unknown cultural links are formed that differ from the existing ones [Ziętek 2002, p. 198]. In the Polish language expressions such as Americanization or McDonaldisation of life, Californication of needs or "the Ikea generation", describing the new social phenomena brought about by globalization, have been functioning successfully already for some time. The tightening of cultural ties on a global scale may be even proven by financial performance in the film industry. *The Avengers*, a Hollywood production of 2012, earned about 625 million USD in the United States and more than 880 million USD outside the U.S. (see Table 5).

Table 5. Proceeds from The Avengers in selected countries (USD million)

China	84.1
United Kingdom	80.6
Mexico	61.8
Australia	54.4
Korea	50.7
Japan	45.3
Russia	43.7

France	37.8
Germany	30.8
Italy	22
Poland	3.2

Source: http://stopklatka.pl/-/35474131,2012-najwieksze-hity-filmowe-w-usa-i-na-swiecie (5.11.2013).

The globalization and the associated multiculturalism affect the growth of social differentiation. On the one hand, the diversity and the use of synergies enable the strengthening of such a society's capacity — on the other hand, however, they can increase animosity and antagonism between different cultural groups. Cooperation and socio-economic exchange on a global scale may be accompanied by the development of isolation, separation or nationalism (see Table 6).

Table 6. Types of multiculturalism

	Multiculturalism type	Relationship Type	Processes	Ideologies
Coexistence	multiplicity diversity individuality	hostility rivalry conflict neutral co-existence	inculturation incorporation	isolationism separation segregation dominance coexistence
Interpenetration and coalescence	multiplicity diversity partial autonomy	interdependence cooperation external pluralism hybridism	integration accommodation acculturation	integrationalism "melting pot" nationalism statism
Structural binding	multiplicity diversity full integration with symbolic separation	integrated social system cultural unity internal pluralism	assimilation unification globalization homogenization	cultural mosaic of unity egalitarism

Source: [Paleczny 2004, p.65–75].

One of the manifestations of globalization is the freedom of movement of all goods, services and people. It is used mainly in businesses, and especially in multinational corporations. They apply the fragmentation of production and strategies for the optimal location, i.e. placing investments and production in these parts of the world where the costs of raw materials and manufacturing are lowest [*Globalizacja gospodarki* 2007, p. 5]. On a global scale, these solutions often stimulate the social and economic inequality. Countries at lower levels of economic development and those rich in deposits of natural resources are exploited without observing the basic principles of care for the environment and human dignity. The disparities in the level and quality of life of the inhabitants of different parts of the world increase. As T. Kaczmarek writes, "contemporary globalization leads to an increase in poverty in all areas of life, especially in the economy, the environment, culture, education and politics. As far as policies are concerned, it is related to lack of democratic principles, disregard for basic civil rights, the lack of equal rights for women, limiting the responsibility of the State and an excessive increase in international structures. In the area of environment protection, poverty is opposed to ecological resources and it is unambiguously stated that the climate is subject to change, that drinking water is becoming less and less accessible, that the ice at the North Pole is melting, and that many species of animals are irretrievably lost. Poverty is also present in the cultural sector, as well as in the availability of education" [Kaczmarek 2013b].

The countries where citizens are forced to sustain themselves for less than 1.25 USD a day include i.a. China (15.9% of the population), Brazil (3.8%), India (41.6%), Mexico (1.8%), Nigeria (64.4%), Egypt (2%), Turkey (2 , 7%) and Bulgaria (1%) (*Rocznik statystyki międzynarodowej* 2012).

Significant differences in the level and quality of life can be seen not only in the traditional division into the developed countries (Europe, United States of America) and the so-called third world countries. They can be seen also within such structure as the European Union: in 2010 the poverty line in Romania was more than 16 times lower than the poverty threshold specified for Germany and Luxembourg (see Table 7 and Figure 1).

Table 7. The poverty threshold in 2010 for households consisting of the indicated number of persons [euro]

Country	1 adult	4 people (2 adults + 2 children under 14 years old)
AT	12,371	25,979
BE	11,678	24,525
BG	1,810	3,801
CY	10,459	21,965
CZ	4,235	8,894
DK	15,401	32,341
EE	3,436	7,216
FI	12,809	26,899
FR	12,027	25,258
GR	7,178	15,073
ES	7,818	16,418
NL	12,175	25,568
IE	13,467	28,281
LT	2,436	5,115
LU	19,400	40,740
LV	2,722	5,717
MT	6,275	13,177

DE	19,438	40,819
PL	2,643	5,551
PT	5,207	10,935
RO	1,222	2,566
SK	3,670	7,707
SI	7,042	14,787
SE	11,825	24,833
HU	2,544	5,343
UK	10,263	21,553
IT	9,562	20,081

Source: [*Rocznik statystyki międzynarodowej* 2012].

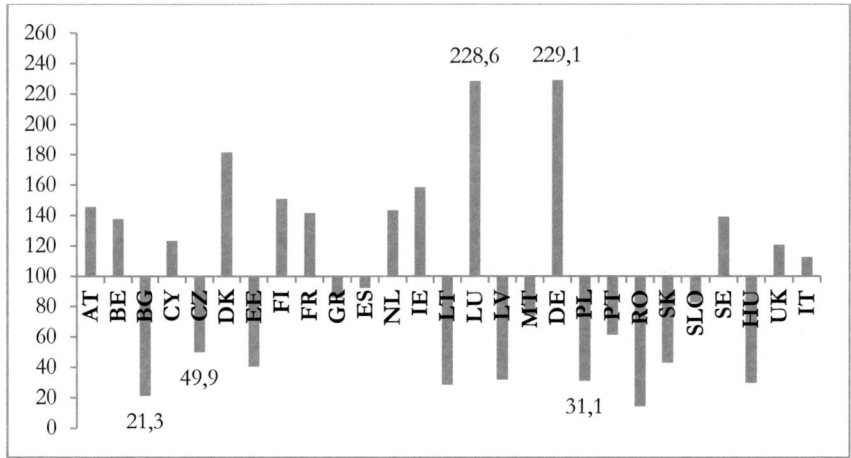

Figure 1. The poverty threshold in single person households in 2010 in comparison to the EU average [EU27 = 100%]
Source: own work on the basis of [*Rocznik statystyki międzynarodowej* 2012].

Globalization certainly gives new opportunities and "opens to the world". Through the use of modern technology even the smallest companies can operate in the global market, the events taking place in other countries can be followed closely and in personal relationships it is possible to maintain familiarity with people from the "other end of the world". Research shows that globalization also leads to isolation and marginalization. Also those who do not want or cannot accept the new conditions are subject to it. The first group includes e.g. senior citizens, for whom their own culture, beliefs, religion and values are something holy, something that should not be communalized, altered, lost. The second group consists of individuals and entire communities which for reasons of economic, social or political nature do not participate in the "global village" on an equal footing.

To sum up the previous considerations, it can be said that globalization is accompanied by a number of socio-economic transformations. These are primarily [Tubielewicz 2000, p. 9]:

— the accelerated development of science and knowledge;
— the construction of coherent international networks of information, research and development;
— the global market and competition, as well as the transfer of technology, goods and funds;
— the global presence of mass media and the Internet;
— the formation of a global information society;
— the migrations and the development of tourism;
— the regional cooperation or confrontation of regional alliances and national states;
— the rapid increase in the number and impact of supranational institutions and organizations;
— the growing sense of dependence between the inhabitants of the globe, leading to the creation of the "global village" vision.

In turn, the effects of global socio-economic transformation in the context of economic development focus on five major trends [Stacewicz 1998, p. 120-123]:

— extending the time horizon of development decisions;
— expanding the scope of development issues to supra-local, cross-regional and supranational contexts;
— changing the primary object of interest changes when making development decisions related to allocation of resources as a result of the fact that from this point of view the natural resources are becoming the main rare good;
— changes in the way of understanding the human being as the subject shaping the processes of development from *homo oeconomicus* to *homo socialis*;
— changes in the selection criteria of development decisions from the "technical criteria" to "quality criteria" (evaluative ones).

The driving force of globalization is the liberalization of trade and financial markets, the growing internationalization of production and distribution strategies of enterprises and the rapid adoption of technologies eliminating barriers to movement of goods, services, capital and people. Economic development is only possible if the countries concerned are able to meet the challenges of globalization associated with the functioning of global financial markets and resulting from the increasing pressures of global competition in goods and services markets [Liberska 2002, p. 324].

1.2. The development of modern technologies

The competitiveness of the economy in the post-industrial civilization depends to a much lesser extent than in case of the earlier civilizations, on the classical factors of production: land, capital and labour. Currently, the dominant role in this area is played by information and knowledge, the skills of using them in practice, as well as by modern technologies.

The literature defines information in rather varied ways. Winer notes that information is the content taken from the outside world, necessary for the individual in the process of its adaptation to such world [Wiener 1961]. According to Berman, information can be analysed in such categories as things, measurable parameters, potential and change [Berman 1991, p. 427]. In turn, Messner associates information with the process of decision-making [Messner 1971].

Unlike in the case of information, the collection and organization of which is more and more frequently entrusted to machines, knowledge is intuitive [Fic 2002, p. 191] and closely associated with the holder [Grudzewski, Hejduk 2004, p. 8] (an individual or an institution). Knowledge is defines "all objectified and established forms of intellectual culture and social awareness, created as a result of accumulation of experiences and learning" [*Encyklopedia Popularna* 1982, p. 849]. Knowledge means the totality of awareness, skills and abilities that can be used by the owner to solve problems[3].

The specific characteristics of knowledge as an economic resource include first of all [*Gospodarka oparta na wiedzy* 2002, p. 18-20]:

— inexhaustibility, which means that unlike in the case of other resources the increased use of knowledge does not cause it to wear out but on the contrary, its value increases,
— volatility – defined as vulnerability to obsolescence,
— simultaneity – related to the fact that the same knowledge can be used by many individuals and organizations at the same time and in many places at once,
— nonlinearity – meaning that even a small amount of knowledge can cause significant consequences, and vice versa: vast amount of knowledge in certain circumstances may be useless,
— immeasurability causing difficulties with a clear definition of the possessed knowledge and placing it in the profit and loss account.

---

[3][Fic 2002, p. 192] – the author refers in the text to the document [*Zarządzanie wiedzą w społeczeństwie uczącym się* 2000, p. 73].

The value of information and knowledge as economic resources depends on the skills and competences of using them in one's activities (see Figure 2).

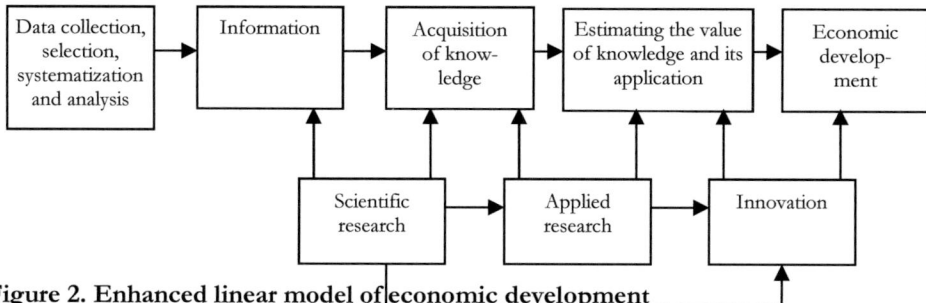

Figure 2. Enhanced linear model of economic development
Source: [*Gospodarka oparta na wiedzy* 2002].

According to the Dictionary of Polish Language a technology is "a method of carrying out a manufacturing or processing process" or "a field of engineering dedicated to the development of new methods of production or processing of raw materials" [*Słownik Języka Polskiego*]. A technology is the practical knowledge of the methods of using resources in production processes associated with the generation of products (goods and services) designed to satisfy specific needs. According to the IDC report, the most important contemporary technologies, in terms of their impact on the level of development of the global economy, are related to information and communication (ICT), new materials and fuels as well as biotechnology and nanotechnology [*Aid to recovery: the economic impact of it, software* 2009].

Modern economy is called the "knowledge-based economy" (KBE) or the "knowledge-driven economy". It's the economy "the operation of which is based on making best use of the knowledge and innovation resources and developing technologies related to fast and cheap access to information" [*Gospodarka oparta na wiedzy* 2002, p. 29]. Its pillars are the technological infrastructure, the human capital (scientific infrastructure), the knowledge management at the organizational level and the social capital [*Gospodarka oparta na wiedzy* 2002, p. 150-162], whilst the modern technologies are its basic "tools". In the European Union mainly the so-called "Old Fifteen" (see Figures 3 and 4) countries can be considered knowledge-based economies.

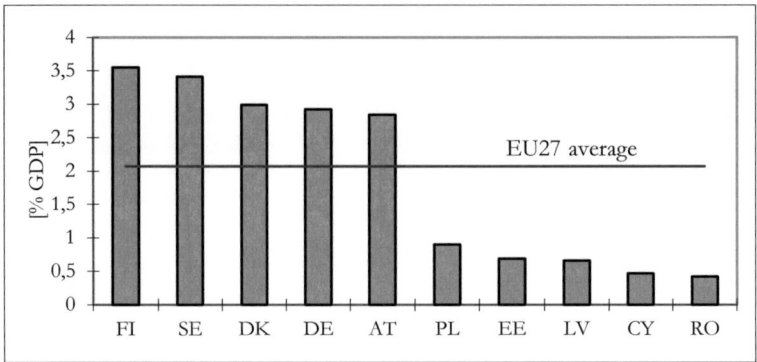

Figure 3. EU countries with the highest and the lowest research and development expenditure in 2012 [%GDP]
Source: own work on the basis of Eurostat data.

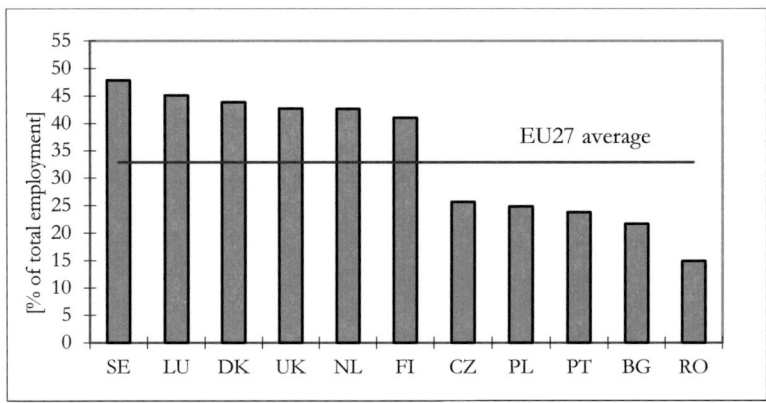

Figure 4. EU countries with the highest and the lowest employment in knowledge-sensitive service sectors in 2008 [% of total employment]
Source: own work on the basis of Eurostat data.

The factors conducive to the development of knowledge-based economy, according to the recommendations of the OECD, are primarily [*Science, Technology and Industrial Outlook* 2000]:

— diffusion of technology and the development of cooperation between research and development centres and enterprises,
— development of technology and innovation policies at national, regional and local level,
— strengthening and reforming the science base,

— implementation of effective incentives supporting research and development activity in enterprises.

The barriers can in turn be grouped into the following categories: systemic, structural, related to awareness and culture, as well as competence-related [Matusiak, Guliński 2010, p. 30-48].

As many authors [Matusiak 2005; Książek, Pruvot 2011] point out, the innovation economy and the development of new technologies, or — more generally — the development of the knowledge economy, depend on the ability to cooperate and use of the diverse potential of many players skilfully. Matusiak says simply that "innovative processes run in a specific arrangement of links, including networks of enterprises, research and development institutions, NGOs and the government, public administration and civil initiatives. The interdependencies that occur between the dynamics of the creation and development of innovative enterprises and the organizations of regions and the availability of specialized support services play an increasing role" [Matusiak 2005]. Table 8 shows the potential partners and the extent of their responsibility for the development of knowledge-based economy.

Table 8. Responsibilities of different actors in shaping the knowledge-based economy

Pillars of KBE	Government	The local authorities	Enterprises		Individuals
			Large	SMEs	
The macroeconomic, legal and institutional infrastructure	Dominant	Significant	Moderate	Moderate	Moderate
The technological Infrastructure	Moderate	Significant	Dominant	Significant	Moderate
The human capital and scientific infrastructure	Dominant	Moderate	Moderate	Significant	Dominant
The knowledge management at the organizational level	Significant	Significant	Dominant	Dominant	Moderate
The social capital	Dominant	Dominant	Moderate	Significant	Moderate

◼ A dominant role (responsibility for) in shaping the KBE conditions
▨ A significant role (responsibility for) in shaping the KBE conditions
☐ A moderate role (responsibility for) in shaping the KBE conditions

Source: [*Gospodarka oparta na wiedzy* 2002, p. 202].

Modern technologies are changing the existing canons in the economy, affecting the behaviour of enterprises and influencing the social behaviour of individuals. The main directions and areas of changes caused by the development of modern technology include [Batorski 2012; Brynjolfsson, McAfee 2011]:

— reprofiling the demand for competences attractive from the point of view of the labour market and a decline in demand for the kinds of work in case of which machines have replaced humans,
— devaluation of meaning the location as a result of dramatic reduction of communication and transport costs,
— implementation of new methods of management and organization of work,
— development of products in digital form.

Modern enterprises aiming at meeting the demands of the contemporary market must be characterized by innovative dynamism and operate the latest technologies effectively. They systematically search for finer and more efficient solutions related to the organization of production, designing new products and applying new forms of selling them, as well as include all groups of employees in the creation of new solutions, continually arousing in them the propensity to innovate [Grudzewski, Hajduk 2005].

1.3. Main trends of demographic changes

Waldziński points to three basic attributes of civilizational changes [Waldziński 2006, p. 141-142]: disappearance of traditionally regarded agencies in charge of economic and social life (economic globalization), mythologisation of reality (belief in modern technology, consumerism) and the cultural chaos. The latter includes the revision of a set of values and norms of social life perpetuated by generations, lifestyles changes and destruction of authorities. The socio-cultural changes observed for several decades and taking place on a global scale seem to drive the chaos. Changing roles of women and men in the family and in society or the liberal approach to family as a social unit are only a few of the causes of the demographic, social and economic effects experienced nowadays and projected for next decades.

The main problem the attention is currently paid to is the accelerated process of population ageing. The number of people of productive age and their share in the total population is steadily decreasing, while the number and share of people of retirement age, including the group of people aged over 80 years, is increasing (see Table 9).

Table 9. Changes in population of Europe in the years 1990–2030 (in thousands)

Years	Age ranges						Total
	0–14	15–24	25–49	50–64	65–79	80+	
1990	148,332	105,324	253,381	124,003	71,868	20,339	723,247
2000	128,192	101,353	269,083	123,071	86,081	21,325	729,105
2010	114,050	94,835	267,139	143,310	89,737	31,237	740,308

| 2020 | 111,967 | 74,200 | 247,903 | 150,563 | 100,120 | 35,862 | 720,615 |
| 2030 | 95,735 | 76,902 | 215,220 | 142,739 | 114,784 | 37,396 | 682,776 |

Source: own work on the basis of [*World Population Prospects* 2013].

According to United Nations estimates, the share of people aged over 50 years in European population will increase from 29.9% in 1990 to 43.2% in 2030. The number of people aged 80 years and over will have increased by over 84% by 2030 in comparison to 1990. In the same period, a significant reduction in the number of people from the youngest group, 0–14 years, shall occur. While in 1990 it accounted for 20.5% of the total population, in 2030 it is supposed to be about 14% (see Figure 5).

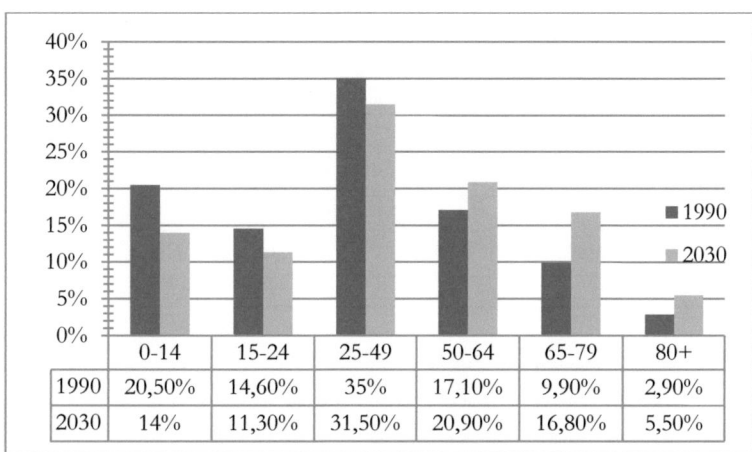

	0-14	15-24	25-49	50-64	65-79	80+
1990	20,50%	14,60%	35%	17,10%	9,90%	2,90%
2030	14%	11,30%	31,50%	20,90%	16,80%	5,50%

Figure 5. The share of age groups in the total population of Europe in the years 1990 and 2030
Source: own work on the basis of [*World Population Prospects* 2013].

Two main reasons for this state of affairs are indicated: the decreasing number of births and the lengthening of the average life span[4].

The decreasing number of births is a result of a number of changes. The most important ones are:

---

[4] According to the Polish Central Statistical Office, the average duration of further life in Poland for men born in 1950 was 56.07 years and 61.68 for women, whereas for children born in 2011, the average duration of further life is estimated to be much longer, respectively, 72.44 years for men and 80.9 years for women [*Przeciętne dalsze trwanie życia* 2013].

— the increase of women's participation in education, including the college and university level (see Table 10) and delaying motherhood — the age of women bearing children rises and the total fertility rate decreases (see Figure 6);
— the increase of women's economic activity in the absence of system solutions enabling women to combine the roles of a mother and a worker [Grzenda 2012; *Podstawowe informacje o sytuacji demograficznej* 2012; Kwiatkowski 2011];
— decreasing authority of the family and its stability and the increasing popularity of lifestyle as a single.

Table 10. Women aged 15 and over by level of education in 2010–2012 [% of total population aged 15 and over holding a given level of education]

	College or university	Postsecondary	Vocational secondary	General secondary	Vocational	Lower secondary, primary and incomplete primary
2010	58.3	73.5	49.1	64.5	39.1	56.9
2011	58.8	72.3	49.0	64.2	38.9	56.7
2012	58.6	72.7	49.3	63.6	38.9	56.6

Source: own work on the basis of [*Aktywność ekonomiczna ludności Polski* 2012].

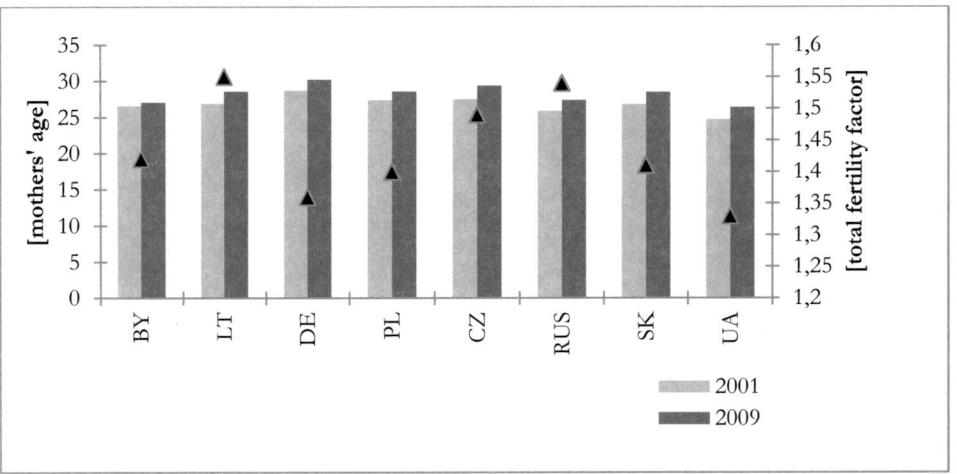

Figure 6. The average age of mothers bearing children in 2001 and 2009 and the total fertility rate in 2009 in Poland and neighbouring countries
Source: own work on the basis of [*Rocznik demograficzny* 2012].

As the research shows, Poles have less and less preference for the traditional family[5] and tend to accept the partnership model[6] more often. More and more young people resign from starting family formation in general and remain single[7]. Szczepański and Jałowiecki point out that the basic features of the Polish singles' lifestyle are "the desire for a career, workaholism, loose sexual relations, postponing the decision to start a family — and especially having children — as well as luxury consumption" [Jałowiecki, Szczepański 2002, p. 298]. Based on the results of research carried out in Poland, singles are categorized as *urban single* [Slany 2008], *metropolitan single* [Czernecka 2008, p. 110-137; Paprzycka 2008] or *metropolitan class* [Jałowiecki, Szczepański 2002].

The ageing of population is also an effect of lengthening the average life span (see Table 11).

Table 11. The average lifespan of EU residents in 2003 and 2012

Country	2003			2012		
	Total	Male	Female	Total	Male	Female
	[years]					
BE	77.6	74.7	80.4	79.9	77.1	82.4
BG	72.2	68.9	75.7	74.0	70.6	77.4
CZ	74.6	71.3	77.8	77.4	74.3	80.4
DK	76.8	74.4	79.1	79.4	77.4	81.4
DE	78.0	75.1	80.6	80.2	77.9	82.6
EE	71.3	65.9	76.6	76.0	70.7	80.9
IE	77.6	75.2	80.0	80.2	78.0	82.4
EL	78.1	75.8	80.5	79.9	77.3	82.6
ES	79.0	75.7	82.3	81.7	78.7	84.7
FR	78.6	75.1	82.0	81.6	78.0	85.0
HR	74.0	70.5	77.5	76.6	73.2	79.9
IT	79.4	76.4	82.1	82.1	79.4	84.5
CY	78.3	76.2	80.5	80.4	78.2	82.6
LV	70.3	65.1	75.3	73.6	68.4	78.3
LT	71.5	65.9	77.1	73.4	67.7	78.9
LU	77.2	74.2	80.2	80.7	78.3	83.0

[5] In 2006, 28% of women and 27% of men preferred the traditional model of marriage. The traditional model of marriage means that "only the husband works, earning enough to meet the needs of the family, while the wife is keeping house and raising children" [*Potrzeby prokreacyjne* 2006, p. 6–8].

[6] In 2006, 47% of women and 35% of men preferred the partnership model of marriage. The partnership model of marriage means that "husband and wife spend about the same amount of time on paid work and both are equally occupied with keeping house and raising children" [*Potrzeby prokreacyjne* 2006, p. 6–8].

[7] The definition of a single most frequently emphasizes that their constitutive feature is the choice of living alone; it is a person who voluntarily decides lead their life in such a way [Stein 1975; Grzeszczyk 2005; Paprzycka 2007].

HU	72.1	67.9	76.2	74.6	70.9	78.1
MT	78.1	76.1	80.0	80.3	78.0	82.5
NL	78.1	75.7	80.3	80.5	78.6	82.3
AT	78.1	75.3	80.8	80.3	77.7	82.8
PL	74.2	70.0	78.3	76.3	72.1	80.5
PT	76.8	73.5	80.1	79.8	76.6	82.9
RO	71.6	68.2	75.2	74.3	70.8	77.9
SK	75.7	71.8	79.6	79.4	76.2	82.5
SI	73.4	69.4	77.3	75.7	72.0	79.3
FI	77.8	74.4	81.2	79.9	76.9	82.9
SE	79.5	77.2	81.7	81.0	79.1	82.8
UK	77.8	75.6	79.9	80.4	78.4	82.3

Source: own work on the basis of Eurostat data.

In Europe, women on average live longer than men. There are clear correlations between the wealth of the state and the lifespan of its citizens (residents of the old and richer countries of the Union live longer than people in the former socialist countries), as well as between geographic and climatic conditions prevailing in the country and the lifespan of people living in it (the people from the southern states statistically live longer even though their countries are in a difficult economic situation).

It is worth emphasizing that in the 2003–2012 period, the average life expectancy rose significantly (approximately two years in each of the surveyed populations) in all European Union countries.

The above-mentioned lifespan increase is influenced by many factors. The most frequently mentioned in the literature include: lengthening of the average lifespan [Polak, Porzych, Kędziora-Kornatowska, Motyl, Porzych, Słupski, Lackowska 2007, p. 51–53], lifestyle (diet, physical and mental activity) and environmental factors (working conditions, the quality of the environment, climate and hygiene) [Zielińska-Więczkowska, Kędziora-Kornatowska, Kornatowski 2007, p. 131–136].

Prevention and modern treatments allow for the preservation of health, as well as physical and mental fitness and increasing lifespan far more effectively than in previous centuries. Older people have better than ever access to medical care, as well are more willing to avail of it. According to statistics of health care services usage the elderly in Poland [*Ochrona zdrowia* 2011]:

— constitute the largest proportion of the hospitalized (in 2010, 32.5% of all the hospitalized were people over 60 years of age);
— avail of medical advice within the framework of the primary healthcare most often (51% of those aged 60–69 years and 65% of those aged 70 years or more

visited their GP at least once during a quarter; in the last quarter of 2010, the elderly patients aged 60 years and more constituted 30% of people availing of primary care physician's advice);

— avail of the long-term domestic care services most frequently (in 2010, persons aged 70 years and over accounted for more than 65% of all patients in the long-term domestic therapeutic services, including over 51% who required multiple home visits).

Moreover, most of the 48% of Poles visiting the pharmacy at least once a month were retirees. 66% of them purchase medical articles in pharmacies at least once a month. They buy prescription and OTC medicines equally often. 17% of OTC medicine buyers are people aged over 60 years [Wdowiak, Lang, Bojar, Kwiatosz-Muc, Owoc 2006, p. 578-582].

Maintaining fitness among seniors and extension of life is also one of the aims of the *active ageing*[8] concept currently being promoted in the European Union. It was introduced in the late 1990s by the World Health Organization (WHO), in relation to the need to stop the increasing exclusion of older people, as a concept of engaging this group and retaining its activity [Kalachea, Kickbusch 1997, p. 4-5]. It is a test of the new approach to ageing and old age. It also shapes a new image of an elderly person. Active ageing "is the process of optimizing opportunities related to health, participation and security, in order to improve the life quality of ageing people" [*Active aging* 2002]. This means the retention of physical fitness and ability to perform work by older people as long as possible, as well as their active participation in social, economic, cultural and civil life. The development of active ageing is determined as much by the external factors as by the internal ones. The external factors determine the environmental conditions in which the elderly operate — i.a. the economic and social factors, the physical environment, health services etc. The internal factors shape mostly the personality of the seniors and their lifestyle [Richert-Kaźmierska, Forkiewicz 2013, p. 128-129].

The ageing process, as an interdisciplinary phenomenon of complex causality and multidimensional effects, will be discussed separately in chapter four of this monograph.

---

[8] More details in: [*Longer working lives* 2009]; [*Council Decision on guidelines for the employment policies* 2003, p. 335]; [*Working together for growth and jobs* 2005, p.10]; [*Opinion of the European Economic and Social Committee on 'Taking into account the needs of older people'* 2007].

References

1. *Active ageing. A policy framework.* World Health Organization, Madrid 2002, http://whqlibdoc.who.int/hq/2002/WHO_NMH_NPH_02.8.pdf (01.02.2011)
2. *Aid to recovery: the economic impact of it, software, and the Microsoft ecosystem on the global economy. White paper*, (2009), IDC Economic Impact Study.
3. *Aktywność ekonomiczna ludności Polski I kwartał 2012r.* (2012), Informacje i opracowania statystyczne, GUS, Warszawa.
4. Ansoff H.I. (1988) *The New Corporate Strategy*, Wiley, New York.
5. Barnet R.J., Cavanagh J. (1994) *Global dreams: imperial corporations and the new world order*, Simon and Schuster, New York.
6. Barber B. (2000) *Globalny dżin*, „Gazeta Wyborcza", 1–2 July.
7. Batorski D. (ed.) (2012) *Cyfrowa gospodarka. Kluczowe trendy rewolucji cyfrowej. Diagnoza, prognozy, strategie reakcji*, Mazowiecka Jednostka Wdrażania Programów Unijnych, Warszawa.
8. Berman C. (1991) *Informacja i aspekty komunikacji*, „Zagadnienia Naukoznawstwa" Nr. 3-4/1991.
9. Bolesta – Kukułka K. (1993) *Jak patrzeć na świat organizacji?*, Wydawnictwo Naukowe PWN, Warszawa.
10. Brynjolfsson E., McAfee A. (2011) *Race Against The Machine: How the Digital Revolution is Accelerating Innovation, Driving Productivity, and Irreversibly Transforming Employment and the Economy*, Digital Frontier Press, Lexington, Massachusetts.
11. *Council Decision on guidelines for the employment policies of the Member States* (2003/578/EC) of 22 July 2003 (OJ EU 2003/ L 197/13).
12. Czernecka J. (2008) *Polski singiel: obraz w mediach a autowizerunek*, (in:) Malinowska E. (ed.), *Stereotypy a rzeczywistość na przykładzie wybranych kategorii społecznych*, Oficyna Wydawnicza TERCJA Łódź.
13. *Encyklopedia Popularna PWN* (1982), PWN, Warszawa.
14. Fic M. (2002) *Rozwój społeczeństwa wiedzy a zmiany w zarządzaniu edukacją* , (in:) *Zarządzanie edukacją a kreowanie społeczeństwa wiedzy*, Politechnika Gdańska Wydział Zarządzania i Ekonomii, Gdańsk.
15. Giddens A. (1997)*Anthony Gibbens on globalization*, UNRISD News No 15.
16. *Globalizacja gospodarki – wybrane cechy procesu* (2007), Departament Analiz i Prognoz, Ministerstwo Gospodarki, Warszawa.
17. *Gospodarka oparta na wiedzy – stan, diagnoza i wnioski dla Polski* (2002), Ekspertyza Instytutu Zarządzania Wiedzą w Krakowie na zlecenie Departamentu Strategii Gospodarczej Ministerstwa Gospodarki. Warszawa-Kraków.
18. Grudzewski W., Hejduk I. (2004), Zarządzanie wiedzą w przedsiębiorstwach, Difin, Warszawa. http://data.worldbank.org/indicator/NY.GDP.MKTP.CD/countries?order=wb

api data value 2012+wbapi data value+wbapi data value-last&sort=asc (9 November 2013).

19. Grudzewski W., Hajduk I. (2005) *Sposoby i techniki zarządzania procesem innowacyjnym. II Konferencja Project Management* – Perspektywy i Doświadczenia.

20. Grzenda W. (2012) *Analiza płodności kobiet w Polsce z wykorzystaniem Bayesowskiego modelu regresji Poissona.* „Przegląd statystyczny", R. LIX, Zeszyt nr 2.

21. Grzeszczyk E. (2005) *Pojedyncze profesjonalistki w Polsce i na świecie.* „Kultura i społeczeństwo" 2/2005.

22. Harris R.G. (1993) *Globalization, trade and income*, "Canadian Journal of Economics".

23. *Indeks globalizacji gospodarek światowych* (2012), http://www.egospodarka.pl/art/galeria/91889,Indeks-globalizacji-gospodarek-swiatowych-2012,1,39,1.html (12.10.2013).

24. Jałowiecki, B., Szczepański, M.S. (2002) *Miasto i przestrzeń w perspektywie socjologicznej*, Wydawnictwo Scholar, Warszawa.

25. Kaczmarczyk M. (2013a) *Niemcy kontra Exxon Mobile*, http://mkaczmarczyk.bblog.pl /tag,budzety;najwiekszych;korporacji;i;panstw,33992.html (6 November 2013).

26. Kaczmarek M. (2013b) *Globalizacja ubóstwa i głodu – próba diagnozy*, http://tarento.nazwa.pl/www-kaczmarek/wp-content/uploads/2012/10/globalizacja_ubostwa.pdf (10 November 2013).

27. Kalachea A., Kickbusch I. (1997) *A global strategy for healthy ageing*, „World Health" (4) July-August 1997.

28. Koźmiński A.K., Jamielniak D. (2011) *Zarządzanie od podstaw*, Oficyna Wolters Kluwer Business, Warszawa.

29. Książek E., Pruvot J.M. (2011) *Budowa sieci partnerstwa i współpracy dla komercjalizacji wiedzy i technologii*, PARP, Poznań-Lille.

30. Kwiatkowski A. (2011) *Czemu w Polsce rodzi się mało dzieci? Diagnoza najważniejszego problemu demograficznego przed jakim stoi współczesna Polska*, Warszawa.

31. Liberska B. (ed.) (2002) *Globalizacja. Mechanizmy i wyzwania*, PWE, Warszawa.

32. *Longer working lives trough pension reform* (2009). Directorate General for Employment , Social Affairs and Equal Opportunities, European Commission, Luxembourg.

33. Matusiak K. (ed.) (2005) *Innowacje i transfer technologii. Słownik pojęć.* PARP, Warszawa.

34. Matusiak K., Guliński J.(ed.) (2010) *System transferu technologii i komercjalizacji wiedzy w Polsce – siły motoryczne i bariery*, PARP, Warszawa.

35. McLuhan M. (1962) *The Gutenberg Galaxy: The Making of Typographic Man*, University of Toronto Press.

36. Messner Z. (1971) *Informacja ekonomiczna a zarządzanie przedsiębiorstwem*, PWN, Warszawa.
37. Michalak W. (1994) *The political economy of trading blocs*, (in:) Gibb R., Michalak W. (ed.) *Continental trading blocs. The growth of regionalism in the world economy*, J.Willey and sons, Chichester.
38. *Ochrona zdrowia w gospodarstwach domowych w 2010 r.* (2011), GUS, Informacje i Opracowania Statystyczne, Warszawa.
39. *Opinion of the European Economic and Social Committee on 'Taking into account the needs of older people'* (OJ EU 2007/C 77/26).
40. Paleczny T. (2004) *Typy tożsamości kulturowej a procesy globalizacji*, (in:) Gorlach K., Niezgoda M., Seręga Z. (ed.), *Władza, naród, tożsamość. Studia dedykowane Profesorowi Hieronimowi Kubiakowi*, Wydawnictwo Uniwersytetu Jagiellońskiego, Kraków.
41. Paprzycka E. (2007) *Jaka jest nowa samotna kobieta?* Materiały Konferencyjne Ogólnopolski Zjazd socjologiczny w Zielonej Górze, 13–15 September 2007.
42. Paprzycka E. (2008) *Kobiety żyjące w pojedynkę. Między wyborem a przymusem*, Państwowe Wydawnictwo Wiedza Powszechna, Warszawa.
43. Piasecki R. (2003) *Rozwój gospodarczy a globalizacja*, PWE, Warszawa.
44. Piskozub A. (2000) *Cywilizacje w czasie i przestrzeni*. UG, Gdańsk.
45. *Podstawowe informacje o sytuacji demograficznej Polski w 2011 roku* (2012), Materiały informacyjne GUS, Warszawa.
46. Polak A., Porzych K., Kędziora-Kornatowska K., Motyl J., Porzych M., Słupski M., Lackowska D. (2007) *Poznawczy i praktyczny wymiar gerontologii – interdyscyplinarnej nauki o starzeniu się i starości*, „Gerontologia Polska" vol. 15, no. 3.
47. *Potrzeby prokreacyjne oraz preferowany i realizowany model rodziny. Komunikat z badań* (2006), CBOS, Warszawa.
48. *Przeciętne dalsze trwanie życia w 2012 roku*, http://www.stat.gov.pl/gus/5840_894_PLK_HTML.htm (12.01.2014).
49. Richert-Kaźmierska A., Forkiewicz M. (2013) *Kształcenie osób starszych w koncepcji aktywnego starzenia się*, (in:) Rączaszek A., Koczur W. (ed.), *Problemy edukacji wobec rozwoju społeczno-gospodarczego*, Studia Ekonomiczne no. 131, Uniwersytet Ekonomiczny w Katowicach, Katowice.
50. Robertson R. (1992) *Globalization – social theory and global culture*, Sage Publication, London,Thousand Oaks, New Deli.
51. *Rocznik demograficzny 2012* (2012), GUS, Warszawa.
52. *Rocznik statystyki międzynarodowej* (2012), GUS Warszawa.
53. *Science, Technology and Industrial Outlook 2000* (2000), Science and Innovation, OECD, Paris 2000.
54. Slany K. (2008), *Alternatywne formy życia małżeńsko-rodzinnego w ponowoczesnym świecie*, Wydawnictwo NOMOS, Kraków.
55. *Słownik Języka Polskiego*, http://sjp.pwn.pl/szukaj/technologia (12 October 2013).

56. *Słownik Wyrazów Obcych* (1991) PWN, Warszawa.
57. Stacewicz J. (1998) *Cywilizacyjno-kulturowy wymiar globalizacji, integracji oraz transformacji*, (in:) Kleer J. (first author), *Globalizacja gospodarki światowej a integracja regionalna. Konsekwencje dla świata i Polski*, Komitet Prognoz „Polska w XXI wieku" PAN, Warszawa.
58. Stein P. (1975) *Singlehood: an alternative to marriage*, „The Family Coordinator", October/1975.
59. Sundram A.K., Black J.S. (1995) *The international business environment. Text and cases.* Prentice-Hall, Englewood Cliffs.
60. Tubielewicz A. (2000) *Globalne uwarunkowania zarządzania*, (in:) Tubielewicz A. (ed.), *Problemy zarządzania i marketingu we współczesnych organizacjach*, WZiE PG, Gdańsk.
61. Waldziński D. (2006) *Skazani na lokalność? Społeczności lokalne wobec ekonomicznych konsekwencji współczesnych przemian kulturowo-cywilizacyjnych*, „Problemy zarządzania" 3/2006.
62. Wdowiak L., Lang B., Bojar I., Kwiatosz-Muc M., Owoc A. (2006) *Self-medication – who buys OTC drugs in Poland?* Zdrowie Publiczne 116(4)/2006.
63. Wiener N. (1961) *Cybernetyka i społeczeństwo*, KiW, Warszawa.
64. Woods N. (ed.) (2000) *The political economy of globalization*, MacMillan Press, London.
65. *Working together for growth and jobs. A new start for the Lisbon Strategy.* Communication to the Spring European Council of 2 February 2005 (COM 2005/24).
66. *World Population Prospects: The 2012 Revision* (2013), United Nations, Department of Economic and Social Affairs, Population Division, Population Estimates and Projections Section, http://esa.un.org/wpp/Excel-Data/population.htm (12.10.2013).
67. Zorska A. (1998), *Ku globalizacji?*, PWN, Warszawa.
68. Zaorska A. (2000) *Ku globalizacji? Przemiany w korporacjach transnarodowych i w gospodarce światowej*, PWN, Warszawa.
69. Zielińska-Więczkowska H., Kędziora-Kornatowska K., Kornatowski T. (2007) *Starość jako wyzwanie*, „Gerontologia Polska" vol. 16, no. 3.
70. Ziętek A. (2002) *Globalizacja a kultura*, (in:) Pietrasia M. (ed.) *Oblicza globalizacji*, Wyd. Uniwersytetu Marii Curie-Skłodowskiej, Lublin.

Chapter II Competitiveness of enterprises in Europe

2.1 The concept of competitiveness and measures of the competitiveness of modern enterprises

Competitiveness is a concept closely related to competition. Grzebyk and Kryński state directly that "competitiveness is an attribute of participants of competition" [Grzebyk, Kryński 2011]. However, while competition is a concept which has been commonly used for a long time, in the sense of competition between rivals[9], and the literature provides many of its definitions [Stankiewicz 2005, p. 19; Noga 1993, p. 23; Jonas 2002, p. 10], competitiveness has been a subject of in-depth research only since the late nineties of the twentieth century.

The concept of competitiveness can be applied to various entities — participants in the competitive struggle. Misala cites i.a. [Misala 2011]:

— competitiveness of products and enterprises (a microeconomic approach),
— competitiveness of industries (a mesoeconomic approach),
— competitiveness of regions and urban areas (a mesoeconomic approach),
— competitiveness of national economies (macroeconomic approach),
— competitiveness of international blocks (megaeconomic approach).

Competitiveness means, in simplified terms, the ability to compete, i.e. operation and survival of an enterprise in the competitive environment [Gorynia, Łaźniewska 2009, p. 51] (see Table 12).

Table 12. Selected definitions of competitiveness

"The ability of a country or an enterprise to create greater wealth than their competitors in the global market"	[*The World Competitiveness Report* 1994, p. 18]
"The ability of enterprises, industries, regions, nations or supranational groups to cope with international competition, as well as to provide a relatively high rate of return on the used factors of production and relatively high employment on a sustainable basis"	[*Globalisation and Competitiveness: Relevant Indicators* 1996, p. 20]
"The ability of the economy to provide residents with high and rising standard of living and a high level of employment on a sustainable basis"	[*European competitiveness report* 2001, p. 19]
"The ability to design, manufacture and sell products (services), the prices, quality and other qualities of which are more attractive than in the case of the corresponding products (services) offered by national and foreign competitors"	[Kisiel 2005, p. 15]

Source: own work.

---

[9] Even though it comes from the Latin word *concurrere,* which literally means *run together.*

Noga proposes several criteria for the division of competitiveness, including: actions or effects, evaluation interval, moment of evaluation, observation time and the level of competitiveness [Noga 1993, p. 37].

The first division allows for distinguishing the process competitiveness (functional approach) and the attribute competitiveness (result-based approach) [Gorynia, Łaźniewska 2009, p. 50]. In the functional approach, attention is drawn to the specific mode of action of an entity, having a decisive influence on its financial results, such as rapid response to changes in the environment, skilful use of own resources, the rationality of decision-making processes etc. Competitiveness in terms of the result-oriented approach determines the results of competition and is measured i.a. among others with market share, financial results, share in sales or the level of innovativeness [Lubiński, Michalski, Misala 1995, p. 9-13].

In the second division Grzebyk and Kryński (2011, p. 113-114] distinguish the operating system and competitiveness. The first means specific technical skills that are essential for the functioning in a given market, while the second refers to the broad context of the competitive behaviour of an entity.

The criterion of assessment moment may be used to distinguish competitiveness *ex ante* and competitiveness *ex post*. The ex post competitiveness according to Gorynia and Łaźniewski [2009, p. 54] is the current competitive position, a kind of a photograph of competitiveness condition at a given time. It is a result of the current confrontation of the competitive strategy implemented by a specified entity and the competitive strategies of its market rivals. On the other hand, competitiveness *ex ante* means the future (prospective) competitive position. It is determined based on the relative (with respect to the leaders of the market) ability of the enterprise to compete in the future. Appointment of competitiveness *ex ante* takes place on the basis of the competitive potential possessed by the entity.

Due to the observation time criterion the static and dynamic competitiveness can be distinguished. According to Stankiewicz [2005, p. 40], static competitiveness is the state of competitiveness of a given entity at a particular moment of time, while dynamic competitiveness consists of changes in the competitiveness of an enterprise within a specified period of time. Gorynia and Łaźniewska add that "competitiveness in the dynamic sense is a set, a string, a sequence of states which capture the static aspect" [Gorynia, Łaźniewska 2009, p. 54]. The authors also propose to equate static competitiveness with the attribute-based competitiveness, while treating the dynamic competitiveness as the equivalent process-based competitiveness.

In the case of modern enterprises, competitiveness is a prerequisite for their survival and growth in the market. It requires an appropriate competitive potential (see Table 13), as well as formulating and implementing competitive strategies [Kisiel 2005, p. 15], observing the actions of competitors and predicting their behaviour [Forlicz 1996, p. 39].

Table 13. The components of the competitive potential of an enterprise

Primary resources	• the entrepreneur's philosophy • know-how • capital necessary to operate
Secondary resources	• material factors of production (fixed assets, materials, raw materials and semi-finished products, means of operation) • human resources • innovations • distribution channels • method of enterprise organization • information
Output resources	• enterprise image (publicity, brand) • the buyers' attitude to products • multiplicity of and the difficulty in overcoming the barriers to switching suppliers identified by existing customers
Other components	• corporate culture • company structure • strategic vision of the company • behaviours specific for the enterprise, including in the field of policy-making;

Source: own work on the basis of [Gorynia, Łaźniewska 2009, p. 55–56].

The measure of competitiveness of an enterprise is its competitive position and competitive advantage in the market.

Competitive position is a result achieved by the enterprise in the process of competition against other market participants, i.e. it is equivalent with the attribute approach to competitiveness. In addition, Gorynia and Łaźniewski [2009, p. 58] treat competitive advantage as a result of implementing a specific competitive strategy against a specific competitive potential and the result of the evaluation of the offer of the enterprise conducted by the market (mainly customers).

Among the indicators used in the assessment of the competitive position of enterprises, the following are usually distinguished:

— market share,
— financial results, with particular emphasis on profitability,

— distinguishing characteristics of the products and services provided by the enterprise,
— recognition of the enterprise in the market, its image among customers and the level of buyer loyalty,
— risk of entry of new competitors or substitute product/service providers.

Competitive advantage, in turn, is the position of an enterprise in its sector in relation to its competitors. The essence of competitive advantage, as Godziszewski [2001, p. 59] writes, boils down to what the enterprise is doing better to achieve better results than its competitors. Achieving competitive advantage by an enterprise is possible by better adapting to market demands [Rutkowski 1997] or possessing certain competences distinguishing it from its competitors [Godziszewski 1997].

Based on the review of the literature it can be concluded that the measurement of enterprise competitiveness is a difficult task, mainly due to the definitional ambiguity of the phenomenon of competitiveness itself and hence the lack of a uniform system of assessment (see Table 14). The most commonly used criteria for measuring competitiveness include:

— resources available to the enterprise, including its distinctive capabilities and core competencies (competitive advantage),
— market acceptance of the enterprise's offering and its continued ability to produce products corresponding to the demand,
— long-term ability to cope with competition (competitive position),
— financial results.

Table 14. Measuring competitiveness – selected perspectives

Category	Measures
Competitive potential of the enterprise	- market share - relative quality - level of service - reputation - acquisition efficiency - speed of execution - mastering the technology - availability of materials
Competitive position	- market position of the enterprise - cost position of the enterprise - brand and market roots - technical competence and mastery of technology - profitability and financial strength
Power of business	- relative market share - absolute market share - relative level of enterprise product quality

	- relative level of selling prices - ratio of expenditures on research and development to sales - ratio of expenditures on marketing to sales
The technological potential	- technical level of products - research and development facilities - quality of production - market share - phase of the life cycle - customer loyalty - know-how
The financial potential	- profitability - liquidity - financial preferences - required level of inventory - financial risk

Source: own work on the basis of [Gorynia, Łaźniewska 2009, p. 77–83].

2.2 The competitiveness of the European economy and the competitiveness of European enterprises

The competitiveness of national economies is an important and current economic problem. The economists and politicians constantly seek to raise the level of competitiveness of national economies. Success in this area, according to Jean [2003, p. 57], allows the citizens to achieve higher profits, and thus increase their personal satisfaction. "A competitive market economy is the only effective solution to the problems and challenges faced by the world economies and societies. The higher the competitiveness of business, region or country, the greater its chance of survival. Lack of competitiveness means exclusion from the market, loss of power over the future and compliance with the dominance of the stronger. The individual and collective economic and social prosperity, the autonomy of the region, as well as the security and independence of the country and the continent depend on the degree of their competitiveness" [*Grupa Lizbońska* 1996, p. 134]. At the same time, excessive concentration on strengthening competitiveness may pose a threat to both the internal policy of the state and the international economic system. According to Krugman, the obsession with competitiveness adversely affects economic policy. Its threats include excessive public expenditure on achieving the wrongly understood competitiveness, increase in state protectionism, trade wars between the largest economic powers, as well as the omission of public policies important from the point of view of the welfare of the citizens [Krugman 1994, p. 30-41].

Among the factors that build the competitiveness of regions and countries, the literature frequently mentions [Piasecki 2003, p. 69-71]:

— the natural resources,
— access to cheap labour,
— favourable macro-economic parameters,
— economic policy implemented by the central government,
— widely understood management methods.

In practice, increasing importance in this regard is attached, however, to access to information, knowledge and modern technology, as well as to the level of intellectual and structural capital of a given region or country. The classic factors of production like land, capital and work [Blaug 2000, p. 300], are steadily losing their importance.

The evaluation of the competitiveness of regional and national economies is conducted by specialized international agencies. The most highly regarded include World Economic Forum (WEF) and Institute for Management Development (IMD). In their analyses the two institutions use a diverse array of criteria (see Table 15) to publish the relevant rankings on the basis of the obtained results. WEF is responsible for the publication of the *Global Competitiveness Report*, the main emphasis of which is the quality of finance, technology, management and operation of the institutions from a given territory[10]. IMD, the creator of the *Global Competitiveness Yearbook*, focuses on an assessment of the central government, internationalisation of economy and population structure[11].

Table 15. Indicators taken into account in the assessment of the competitiveness of economies

World Economic Forum	Institute for Management Development
— openness of the economy — central government — financials — infrastructure — technology — management — labour — institutions	— national economy — internationalisation of the economy — assessment of the central government — financials — infrastructure — management of enterprises — science and technology — population

[10] www.weforum.org
[11] www.imd.ch

Source: own work on the basis of World Economic Forum data and Institute for Management Development data.

According to the *Global Competitiveness Report 2013-2014* [Schwab 2013], all economies of the world are divided into three main groups (see Table 16):
— resource-based factor-driven economies;
— modern, efficiency-driven economies;
— competitive, innovation-driven economies.
The countries belonging to the first group compete using their natural resources and unskilled, cheap labour. The countries classified as efficiency-driven economies are characterized by the development of modern, efficient methods of production and the increasing quality of offered products and services. Their competitive advantage is based on the education of their citizens, effective labour market solutions, investments in modern technologies, as well as security of the financial markets. The third group of countries includes the most developed and competitive economies. They are characterized by a high quality of life, a high level of entrepreneurial development, the availability of new, innovative products, as well as the use of modern methods of production.

The list includes also the countries in transition, i.e. being in the course of changing groups. Poland can be an example of such country, as in the *Global Competitiveness Report in 2013-2014* it was assessed as a state evolving from efficiency-driven to innovation-driven economy.

Table 16. Classification of world economies according to their competitive advantages

Factor-driven economies	Transition from factor-driven economy to efficiency-driven economy	Efficiency-driven economies	Transition from efficiency-driven economy to innovation-driven economy	Innovation-driven economies
Bangladesh	Algeria	Albania	Argentina	Australia
Benin	Angola	Bosnia and Herzegovina	Barbados	Austria
Burkina Faso	Armenia	govina	Brazil	Bahrain
Burundi	Azerbaijan	Bulgaria	Chile	Belgium
Cambodia	Bhutan	Cape Verde	Costa Rica	Canada
Cameroon	Bolivia	China	Croatia	Cyprus
Chad	Botswana	Colombia	Estonia	Czech Republic
Cote d'Ivoire	Brunei Darussalam	Dominican Republic	Hungary	Denmark
Ethiopia	Gabon	Ecuador	Kazakhstan	Finland
Gambia	Honduras	Egypt	Latvia	France
Ghana	Iran	El Salvador	Lebanon	Germany
Guinea	Kuwait	Georgia	Lithuania	Greece
Haiti	Libya	Guatemala	Malaysia	Hong Kong
India	Moldova	Guyana	Mexico	Iceland

Kenya	Mongolia	Indonesia	Panama	Ireland
Kyrgyz Re-	Morocco	Jamaica	Poland	Israel
public	Philippines	Jordan	Russian Federa-	Italy
Lao PDR	Saudi Arabia	Macedonia	tion	Japan
Lesotho	Sri Lanka	Mauritius	Seychelles	Korea, Rep.
Liberia	Venezuela	Montenegro	Slovak Republic	Luxemburg
Madagascar		Namibia	Turkey	Malta
Malawi		Paraguay	Uruguay	Netherlands
Mali		Peru		New Zealand
Mauritania		Romania		Norway
Mozambique		Serbia		Portugal
Myanmar		South Africa		Puerto Rico
Nepal		Suriname		Qatar
Nicaragua		Swaziland		Singapore
Nigeria		Thailand		Slovenia
Pakistan		Timor-Leste		Spain
Rwanda		Tunisia		Sweden
Senegal		Ukraine		Switzerland
Sierra Leone				Taiwan, China
Tanzania				Trinidad and
Uganda				Tobago
Vietnam				United Arab
Yemen				Emirates
Zambia				United Kingdom
Zimbabwe				United States

Source: [Schwab 2013, p. 11].

In the Institute for Management Development *Global Competitiveness Yearbook 2013* [*The World Competitiveness Scoreboard* 2013] Poland was classified as 33rd world economy in terms of competitiveness[12] with a score of 65.437 points (out of 100 points available).

Table 17. Most competitive economies in the world in 2013 according to the Institute for Management Development

Place in the 2013 ranking	Country	Place in the 2012 ranking
1.	United States of America	2
2.	Switzerland	3
3.	Hong Kong	1
4.	Sweden	5
5.	Singapore	4
6.	Norway	8
7.	Canada	6
8.	United Arabian Emirates	16

---

[12] The ranking takes into account 60 world economies.

9.	Germany	9
10.	Quatar	10
11.	Taiwan	7
12.	Denmark	13
13.	Luxembourg	12
14.	Netherlands	11
15.	Malaysia	14
16.	Australia	15
17.	Ireland	20
18.	United Kingdom	18
19.	Israel	19
20.	Finland	17
21.	China Mainland	23
22.	Korea	22
23.	Austria	21
24.	Japan	27
25.	New Zealand	24
26.	Belgium	25
27.	Thailand	30
28.	France	29
29.	Iceland	26
30.	Chile	28
31.	Lithuania	36
32.	Mexico	37
33.	Poland	34
34.	Kazakhstan	32
35.	Czech Republic	33
36.	Estonia	31
37.	Turkey	38
38.	Philippines	43
39.	Indonesia	42
40.	India	35

Source: [*The World Competitiveness Scoreboard* 2013].

Most Member States of the European Union (mainly the so-called "Old fifteen") are now included in the most competitive economies in the world. Since the beginning of the integration processes taking place in Europe, the ambition of European politicians was to make the EU economy at least as competitive as the economy of the United States. Such intention was expressly included in the *Lisbon Strategy* in 2000. In the document programming economic development of the European Union for the next decade, the main economic purpose was described by the heads of governments of the "Fifteen" as follows: The European Union should become the most competitive and dynamic knowledge-based economy in the world, capable of sustainable economic growth and offering more and better jobs and greater social cohesion [*Lisbon European Council* 2000]. Enhancing competitiveness and attractiveness of Europe as a place to live, work and invest are the main objectives of the European Union strongly emphasized also in the *Renewed Lisbon Strategy* [*Common actions for growth and employment* 2005], as well is the *Europe 2020* [2010] document.

The pursuit of high competitiveness of the EU economy requires the activity of both politicians in Brussels and the authorities of the Member States and their regions in a number of areas: the internal market, the creation of the information society, the development of scientific research, investment in education, the implementation of structural economic reforms, stable currency and series of macroeconomic moves for growth and sustainability of public finances. During the economic crisis of the first decade of the twenty-first century, the key actions were identified in five areas [*European competitiveness report* 2012]:

— the creation and development of value chains on a global scale;
— increasing energy efficiency as a determinant of export attractiveness of the goods;
— better use of the potential of foreign direct investments;
— building and strengthening of existing co-operation networks, i.e. clusters and other forms of interaction in business;
— optimizing the benefits resulting from the European Single Market freedoms.

The pillars of the competitiveness of the EU economy include entrepreneurship and innovation, mainly in the small and medium-sized enterprises sector. A declaration in this regard was adopted by all Member States in the form of *European Charter for Small Enterprises* [2004]. In the preface by the Commissioner for Enterprise and the Information Society, we read: "Implementation of the strategic recommendations of the Charter is essential for achieving the Lisbon objective of making Europe the most competitive and dynamic economy in the world" [*European Charter for Small Enterprises* 2004, p. 4].

As the results of the report for the years 2011/2012 show [*EU SMEs* 2012], the situation of SMEs in Europe and their competitiveness is slowly improving despite the still difficult macroeconomic situation. The SME sector[13] represents approximately 99.8% of all European businesses, i.e. approximately 21 million enterprises. The vast majority of them are micro-enterprises employing up to 9 individuals (see Table 18).

---

[13] In EU statistics three classes of SMEs are distinguished: micro enterprises, small- and medium scale enterprises. Micro enterprises are enterprises that employ up to 9 people. Small enterprises employ between 10 and 49 people. Medium enterprises employ between 50 and 249 people. Large enterprises are thus defined as having 250 or more employees.

The SME sector is a major European employer, creating almost 70% of all jobs in the European Union.

Table 18. Enterprises in the European Union in 2012 – basic statistics

	Micro	Small	Medium	SMEs	Large	Total
Number of enterprises						
Number	19,143,521	1,357,533	226,573	20,727,627	43,654	20,771,281
%	92.2	6.5	1.1	99.8	0.2	100
Employment						
Number	38,395,819	26,771,287	22,310,205	87,477,311	42,318,854	129,796,165
%	29.6	20.6	17.2	67.4	32.6	100
Gross value added						
EUR millions	1,307,360.7	1,143,935.7	1,136,243.5	3,587,540	2,591,731.5	6,179,271.4
%	21.2	18.5	18.4	58.1	41.9	100

Source: [EU SMEs 2012].

The basic criterion for the assessment of the competitiveness of enterprises in Europe is their productivity, employment potential and the ability to generate added value. In addition, attention is paid to innovativeness of enterprises, and whether they operate in knowledge-based sectors. The statistical data indicate that due to the latter of these criteria, the majority of EU businesses still represents an insufficiently satisfactory level of competitiveness (see Table 19) and requires support.

Table 19. Number and share of enterprises by technology and knowledge base by size-class in EU-27 in 2011 (estimates)

	SMEs		Large enterprises	
	Number of enterprises	% share of total SMEs	Number of enterprises	% share of large enterprises
Manufacturing				
High-tech (HTM)	45,871	0.2	1,141	2.6
Medium-high-tech (MHTM)	192,980	0.9	5,136	11.8
High+Medium-high-tech (HMHTM)	238,851	1.2	6,277	14.4
Medium-low-tech (MLTM)	691,096	3.3	4,305	9.9
Low-tech (LTM)	1,060,868	5.1	5,399	12.4
Services				
Knowledge intensive services (KIS)	4,316,746	20.9	7,483	17.2
Knowledge-intensive market services (KIMS)	3,416,703	16.5	5,057	11.6
High-tech knowledge-intensive services (HKIS)	749,904	3.6	1,888	4.3
Other knowledge-intensive services (OKIS)	150,139	0.7	538	1.2

Low knowledge-intensive services (LKIS)	11,101,425	53.6	15,999	36.8

Source: [*EU SMEs* 2012].

In order to strengthen the innovativeness of EU enterprises, and thus improve their competitiveness, the European Commission launches special support programs. For 2007–2013, the Framework Programme and the Competitiveness and Innovation Programme (CIP) was created, especially for small and medium-sized enterprises (SMEs) — it aims at supporting innovation activities (including eco-innovation), as well as providing better access to finance and support services for business at the regional level. The program also aims at promoting a wider and better use of information and communication technologies (ICT) and supporting the development of the information society. The programme also promotes the increased use of renewable energy and energy efficiency[14]. Strengthening the competitive potential of European companies, and as a result their competitive advantage over companies from other parts of the world, is also one of the aims of the Seventh Framework Programme (FP7), implemented in the period 2007–2013. FP7 provides financial support for transnational research conducted by SMEs. Strengthening the innovation and competitiveness of EU enterprises is to be based on three primary components of FP7: Cooperation, People and Capacities [*SMEs in FP7* 2007].

For the 2014–2020 programming period, the European Commission has prepared another program dedicated to SMEs wishing to raise their competitiveness – COSME **(Programme for the Competitiveness of Enterprises and SMEs). The recipients of the program are** mainly entrepreneurs who will benefit from easier access to funds for their business operations, citizens having problems with establishing and running their own businesses, as well as the authorities of the EU Member States, which will have better support for efforts aimed at developing and implementing effective policy reforms. The programme aims at facilitating access to finance for SMEs, creating a suitable environment conducive to the creation of new enterprises, encouraging entrepreneurship in Europe, strengthening of the competitiveness of the European economy, as well as promoting the internationalization of SMEs[15]. One of the main tasks foreseen within the framework of COSME is developing the *Entrepreneurship Action Plan 2020*, a joint programme implemented at EU, national, regional and local levels. It is to be focused on three areas: entrepreneurship education, creation of an environment favourable for entrepreneurs (mainly within the dimensions of legislation, taxation, access to advisory services and provision of on-line service for

---

[14] http://ec.europa.eu/cip/index_pl.htm (12.12.2013).
[15] http://ec.europa.eu/enterprise/initiatives/cosme/index_en.htm (12.12.2013).

entrepreneurs) and the development of forms of supporting entrepreneurial attitudes among young people, women and the elderly.

2.3 The competitiveness of Polish enterprises

Polish economy, although its macroeconomic condition seems to be relatively favourable, against the background of the European economy is seen as less competitive. Throughout the period of the recent global economic crisis, i.e. in the years 2007–2013, Poland was the only EU country that did not fall into recession — it also has a very optimistic forecast for 2014 (see Table 20).

Table 20. Macroeconomic forecasts for the European Union for the year 2014

	Economic growth [%]		Unemployment rate[16] [%]		Budget surplus/deficit [% GDP]	
Top five economies in the EU in 2014	LV	4.1	AT	5	**PL**	**4.6**
	LT	3.6	DE	5.5	DE	0.1
	EE	3	MT	6.3	EE	-0.1
	SE	2.8	LU	6.4	LU	-1.0
	PL	**2.5**	CZ	7	LV	-1.0
EU average	**1.4**		**11**		**- 2.7**	

Source: own work on the basis of [Niedziński 2014].

The poor rating of our economy's competitiveness is affected i.a. by the low economic activity of Poles, low productivity of enterprises, unsatisfactory level of enterprise innovation and underdeveloped networks of cooperation between science and business, as well as complex and unstable legal rules. The deficit of capital investment in infrastructure and modernization of the technologies used by enterprises, the lack of a strategy for the transfer of technologies and the general lack of adaptation to the requirements of modern knowledge-based economy are, in turn, the causes of the Polish enterprises' fundamental inability of effective participation in competition with companies from more developed European countries [Geodecki 2012].

Overview of the Polish literature related to the competitiveness of enterprises fails to provide clear answers on what should be done in order for the Polish enterprises to become increasingly competitive in the European and world markets, how it should be done and who should take the necessary actions. Skawińska [2002, p. 83-95] indicates that the competitiveness of enterprises is formed by four groups of factors: sources of competitive advantage, the potential of competitiveness, instruments of competition and the environment in which the enterprise operates (see Figure 7).

---

[16] The unemployment rate projected for Poland for 2014 is 10.8%.

Kaya [1996, p. 96-175] draws attention to the crucial importance of enterprise architecture, its innovativeness, as well as its distinctive capabilities in the form of reputation. Pomykalski [2008, p. 304-306] considers the level of competitiveness of an enterprise to be determined by its ability to generate two types of values, namely: customer value and shareholder value. To sum up, it can be said that the keys to the success of modern enterprises are customer satisfaction and maximizing shareholder value. Obłój [2010] contends, on the other hand, that the basis for functioning of each enterprise, including the achievement of its competitive advantage, is the skilful management. According to this author, the company should continuously manage and improve its business operations. This requires discipline, which helps to achieve planned results and operate effectively.

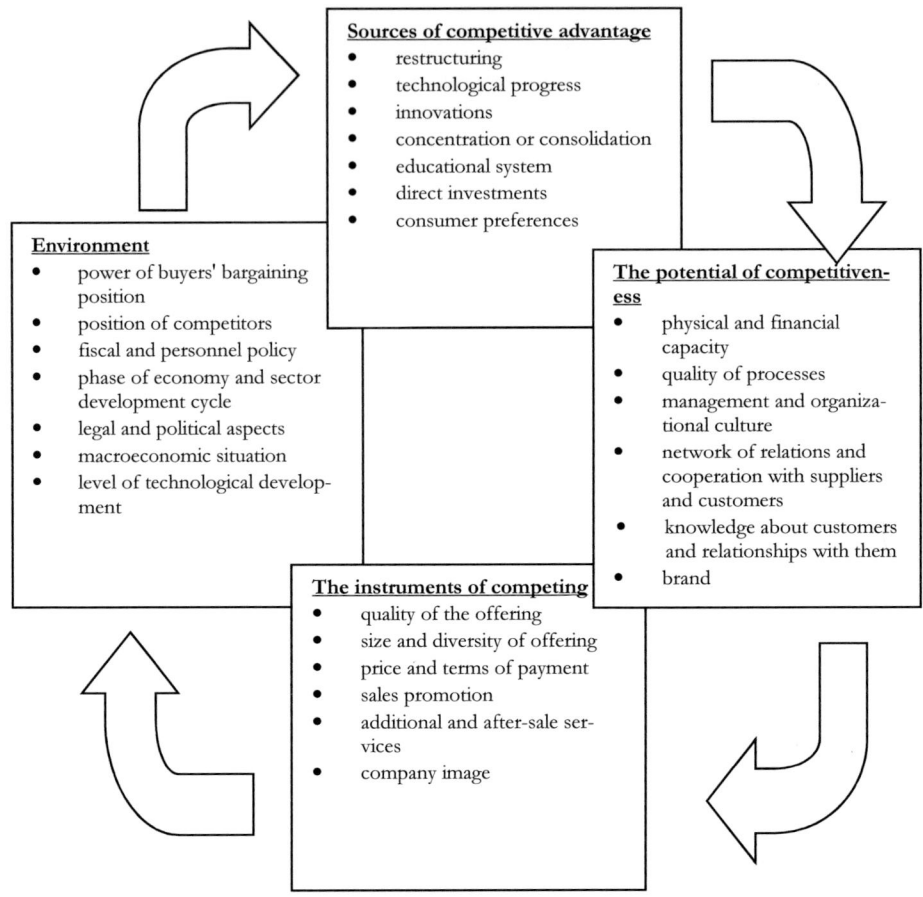

Sources of competitive advantage
- restructuring
- technological progress
- innovations
- concentration or consolidation
- educational system
- direct investments
- consumer preferences

Environment
- power of buyers' bargaining position
- position of competitors
- fiscal and personnel policy
- phase of economy and sector development cycle
- legal and political aspects
- macroeconomic situation
- level of technological development

The potential of competitiveness
- physical and financial capacity
- quality of processes
- management and organizational culture
- network of relations and cooperation with suppliers and customers
- knowledge about customers and relationships with them
- brand

The instruments of competing
- quality of the offering
- size and diversity of offering
- price and terms of payment
- sales promotion
- additional and after-sale services
- company image

Figure 7. Groups of factors shaping the competitiveness of enterprises
Source: own work on the basis of [Skawińska 2002, p. 83–95].

As in other European Union Member States, the SMEs dominate in the Polish economy (accounting for 99.8% of all businesses). However, compared with the EU average, the Polish SME sector is increasingly dominated by micro-enterprises[17], whose share in the total number of companies amounts to 95.9% [Tarnawa, Zadurska-Lichota 2013] (see Table 21).

---

[17] For statistical purposes, the Central Statistical Office divides companies into four size classes due to the number of employees: micro (0–9), small enterprises (10–49), medium-sized enterprises (50–249) and large enterprises (250 and more).

Table 21. Number of enterprises active in Poland in different size classes in 2011 (thousands)

	Total	Micro-enterprises	Small enterprises	Medium-sized enterprises	Large companies
The number of enterprises	1,784.6	1,710.6	55.0	15.8	3.2
% of the total number of enterprises	100	95.9	3.1	0.9	0.1

Source: own work on the basis of [Tarnawa, Zadura-Lichota 2013, p. 20].

SMEs operating in Poland generate almost 71.8% of Polish GDP and create 70.2% of all jobs. The biggest employers in Poland are micro-enterprises run by sole traders and large companies, created by legal persons (see Figure 8). Employment in enterprises is much lower than the number of the working, mainly in the group of micro-enterprises. Such structure of employment is shaped i.a. by a high percentage of sole traders who do not employ anyone.

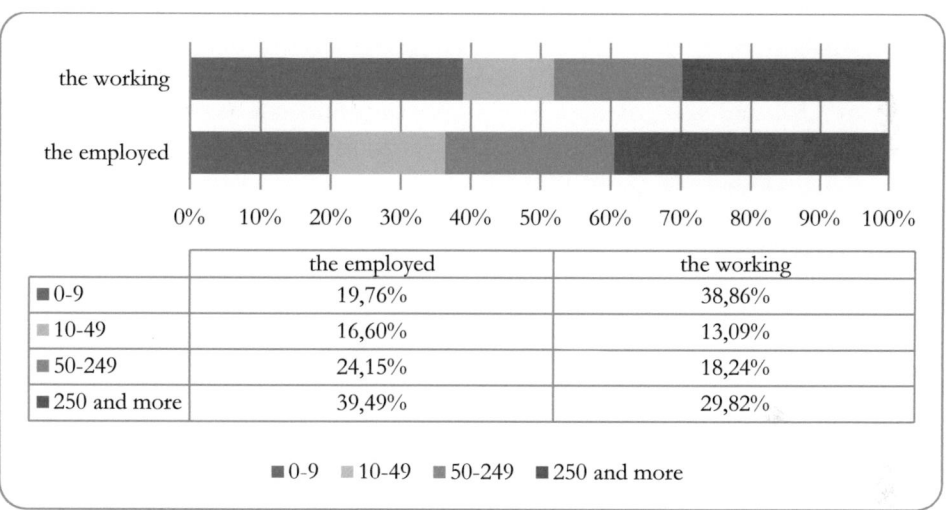

	the employed	the working
■ 0-9	19,76%	38,86%
■ 10-49	16,60%	13,09%
■ 50-249	24,15%	18,24%
■ 250 and more	39,49%	29,82%

■ 0-9 ■ 10-49 ■ 50-249 ■ 250 and more

Figure 8. The structure of the number of the working and the employed in enterprises in Poland in 2011
Source: [Tarnawa, Zadura-Lichota 2013, p. 34].

In Poland, most of the SMEs conduct operations related to services (46.5%), trade (29.5%) and construction (13.4%). Fewer undertakings of this type of deal with industrial activity (only 10.6%). In the group of large enterprises the situation is quite different. The largest group consists of industrial enterprises (52.8%), while service and trade enterprises are rarer (28.1% and 13.5%, respectively).

Polish SMEs are much weaker economically than companies from the other EU countries. They have a smaller share in the added value (see Table 22) and are characterized by a less favourable revenue growth. The productivity of enterprises in Poland per employee or per company is clearly lower than the average in the European Union. According to the company turnover per employee, Polish enterprises occupy the 21th place in the ranking of 26 European countries. Polish entities have also a similar position in rankings related to production and added value per employee.

Table 22. Structure of gross value added in the business sector by size of enterprises in Poland and the European Union in 2010

Size of enterprise	Poland	EU-28
	[%]	
Micro	15.9	21.2
Low	13.2	18.2
Average	21.5	18.2
High	49.4	42.4

Source: [Tarnawa, Zadura-Lichota 2013, p. 38].

The improvement in the assessment of the competitiveness of Polish companies in the coming years could be affected by investment growth. According to CSO data, in 2011 the investments in the SME sector increased in comparison with the previous year by 13% and reached 80 billion PLN. Unfortunately, most of the investments were realized using the enterprises' own funds (more than 60% of the total). This means that dominating forms of investment were tactical, low-cost and relatively less innovative. Companies forming the largest group (the micro and small ones) still invest very little. The investment outlays are growing mainly in medium-sized and large enterprises (14.1% and 13.9% compared to 2010, respectively).

In addition, increasing the competitiveness of Polish enterprises is fostered by such factors as:

— the implementation of active innovation policy and increased spending on research and development [Geodecki 2012],
— development of cooperation between enterprises and business institutions, as well as enterprises and research centres [Dzierżanowski 2012],
— increasing the flexibility of the management of enterprises, so that they are able to quickly and efficiently react to changes in their environment [Kasewicz, Ormińska, Rogowski, Urban 2009],
— simplification of procedures relating to the establishment and operation of enterprises [Kostrubiec, Szczęśniak, Zdyb 2013],

— increasing the availability of EU funds (also by procedural and managerial improvements) for enterprises intending to grow their business through the implementation of innovative solutions [*Polityka spójności UE na lata 2014-2020*],
— structural changes in the corporate sector and changes of attitudes and motivations of entrepreneurs regarding the development of their enterprises (see Figure 9).

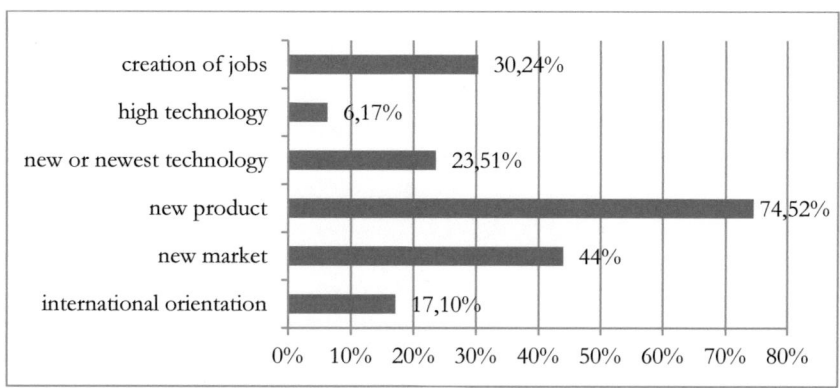

Figure 9. Entrepreneurial aspirations of Polish entrepreneurs (entrepreneurial attitudes and perception of entrepreneurship)
Source: [Zbierowski 2012, p.37].

References

1. Blaug M. (2000) *Teoria ekonomii. Ujęcie retrospektywne*, Wydawnictwo Naukowe PWN, Warszawa.
2. *Common actions for growth and employment. A new start for the Lisbon strategy* (2005), Communication to the spring European Council, COM (2005) 24 final, Brussels, 2.2.2005.
3. Dzierżanowski M. (ed.) (2012) *Kierunki i założenia polityki klastrowej w Polsce do 2020 roku*, Rekomendacje Grupy roboczej ds. polityki klastrowej, PARP, Warszawa.
4. *Europe 2020 strategy for smart, sustainable and inclusive growth* (2010), Communication from the Commission, COM(2010) 2020 final, Brussels, 3.3.2010.
5. *European competitiveness report 2001* (2001), European Commission, Luxembourg.
6. *European competitiveness report 2012. Reaping the benefits of globalization*, Commission Staff Working Document SWD(2012)299 final accompanying document to the Communication from the Commission A stronger European Industry for Growth and Economic Recovery Industrial Policy Communication Update COM(2012)582 final, http://ec.europa.eu/enterprise/policies/industrial-competitiveness/competitiveness-analysis/european-competitiveness-report/files/ecr2012_full_en.pdf (12.12.2013).
7. *EU SMEs in 2012: at the crossroads* (2012), Annual report on small and medium-sized enterprises in the EU, 2011/12, Ecorys for European Commission, Rotterdam.
8. Forlicz S. (1996) *Mikroekonomiczne aspekty przepływu informacji między podmiotami rynkowymi*, Wydawnictwo WSB w Poznaniu, Poznań.
9. Geodecki T. (first author) (2012) *Kurs na innowacje. Jak wyprowadzić Polskę z rozwojowego dryfu?* Fundacja Gospodarki i Administracji Publicznej, Kraków.
10. *Globalisation and Competitiveness: Relevant Indicators* (1996), "STI Working Papers" no. 5, OECD, Paris.
11. Godziszewski B. (1997) *Umiejętności firmy jako podstawa trwałej przewagi konkurencyjnej*, (in:) Borowiecki R. (ed.), *Restrukturyzacja i konkurencyjność przedsiębiorstw*, Akademia Ekonomiczna w Krakowie, Zakopane.
12. Godziszewski B. (2001), *Zasobowe uwarunkowania strategii przedsiębiorstwa*, UMK, Toruń.
13. Gorynia M., Łaźniewska E. (2009) *Kompendium wiedzy o konkurencyjności*, PWN, Warszawa.
14. *Grupa Lizbońska: Granice konkurencji* (1996), Poltext, Warszawa.
15. Grzebyk M., Kryński Z. (2011) *Konkurencja i konkurencyjność przedsiębiorstw. Ujęcie teoretyczne*, (in:) Woźniak M.G.(red.), *Nierówności społeczne a wzrost gospodarczy. Uwarunkowania sprawnego działania w przedsiębiorstwie i regionie*, Zeszyt nr 20, Wydawnictwo Uniwersytetu Rzeszowskiego, Rzeszów.

16. http://www.weforum.org
17. http://www.imd.ch
18. http://ec.europa.eu/cip/index_pl.htm
19. http://ec.europa.eu/enterprise/initiatives/cosme/index_en.htm
20. *Institute for Management Development,* http://www.imd.ch/research/publications /wcy/index.cfm (10.10.2013).
21. Jean C. (2003) *Gopolityka,* Ossolineum, Wrocław-Warszawa-Kraków.
22. Jonas A. (2002) *Strategie konkurencji na rynku usług bankowych,* Biblioteka menedżera i bankowca, Warszawa.
23. Kay J. (1996) *Podstawy sukcesu firmy,* PWE, Warszawa.
24. Kasewicz S., Ormińska J., Rogowski W., Urban W. (2009) *Metody osiągania elastyczności przedsiębiorstw. Od zarządzania zasobowego do procesowego,* Oficyna Wydawnicza SGH, Warszawa.
25. Kisiel M. (2005) *Internet a konkurencyjność banków w Polsce,* CeDeWu, Warszawa.
26. Kostrubiec J., Szczęśniak P., Zdyb M. (ed.) (2013) *Prawno-administracyjne ograniczenia podejmowania i prowadzenia działalności gospodarczej,* Wydział Prawa i Administracji UMCS, Lublin.
27. Krugman P. (1994) *Competitiveness: a dangerous obsession,*"Foreign Affairs" 73, No. 2/1994.
28. *Lisbon European Council, 23 and 24 March 2000. Presidency conclusions.* http://www.europarl.europa.eu/summits/lis1_en.htm (10.12.2013).
29. Lubiński M., Michalski T., Misala J. (1995) *Międzynarodowa konkurencyjność gospodarki. Pojęcia i sposób mierzenia,* Instytut Rozwoju i Studiów Strategicznych, Warszawa.
30. Misala J. (2011) *Międzynarodowa konkurencyjność gospodarki,* PWE, Warszawa.
31. Niedziński B., *KE: Polska znajdzie się wśród unijnych liderów wzrostu PKB,* http://forsal.pl/artykuly/ 768264,ke-polska-znajdzie-sie-wsrod-unijnych-liderow-wzrostu-pkb.html (2.01.2014).
32. Noga A. (1993) *Dominacja a efektywna konkurencja,* SGH Warszawa.
33. Obłój K. (2010) *Pasja i dyscyplina strategii. Jak z marzeń i decyzji zbudować sukces firmy,* Poltext, Warszawa.
34. Piasecki R. (2003) *Rozwój gospodarczy a globalizacja,* PWE, Warszawa.
35. *Polityka spójności UE na lata 2014–2020. Ukierunkowanie inwestycji na działania wspierające wzrost gospodarczy,* http://ec.europa.eu/regional_policy/sources/docgener/informat/2014/fiche_s me_pl.pdf (02.01.2014).
36. Pomykalski A. (2008) *Zmiany strategiczne a konkurencyjność przedsiębiorstw na rynku globalnym,* (in:) Kaleta A., Moszkowicz K. (ed.), *Zarządzanie strategiczne w badaniach teoretycznych i w praktyce,* Prace Naukowe Uniwersytetu Ekonomicznego we

Wrocławiu, no. 20, Wydawnictwo Uniwersytetu Ekonomicznego we Wrocławiu, Wrocław.

37. Rutkowski I. (1997) *Marketing jako źródło przewagi konkurencyjnej na rynku* (in:) *Marketing jako czynnik i instrument konkurencji*, PWE, Warszawa.
38. Schwab K. (2013) *The Global Competitiveness Report 2013–2014. Full Data Edition.* Insight Report. World Economic Forum, Geneva.
39. Skawińska E. (2002) *Konkurencyjność przedsiębiorstw - nowe podejście*, PWN, Warszawa-Poznań.
40. *SMEs in FP7. Guide* (2007), Office for Official Publications of the European Communities, Luxembourg.
41. Stankiewicz M.J. (2005) *Konkurencyjność przedsiębiorstwa* (in:) *Budowanie konkurencyjności przedsiębiorstwa w warunkach globalizacji*, Dom Organizatora, Toruń.
42. Tarnawa A., Zadura-Lichota P. (ed.) (2013) *Raport o stanie sektora małych i średnich przedsiębiorstw w Polsce w latach 2011 - 2012*, PARP, Warszawa.
43. *The European Charter for Small Enterprises* (2004), Annex III to the Conclusions of the Presidency of the Santa Maria Da Feira European Council of 19 and 20 June 2000, Office for Official Publications of the European Communities, Luxembourg.
44. *The World Competitiveness Report 1994* (1994), World Economic Forum, Lausanne.
45. *The World Competitiveness Scoreboard* (2013), http://www.imd.org/uupload/ IMD.WebSite/wcc/WCYResults/1/scoreboard.pdf (22.12.2013).
46. *World Economic Forum,* http://www.weforum.org/en/initiatives/gcp/Global %20Competitiveness %20Report/index.htm (10.10.2013).
47. Zbierowski P. (first author) (2012) *Global Entrepreneurship Monitor. Poland*, Polska Agencja Rozwoju Przedsiębiorczości, Warszawa.

Chapter III Innovation and innovativeness of competing enterprises

3. 1. The contemporary meaning of the concepts of innovation and innovativeness

The concept of innovation has been defined in many ways but many of them were inspired by J.A. Schumpeter's [Schumpeter 1934] proposal, describing innovation as a specific combination of knowledge and other resources deployed in practice. In the Schumpeterian theory five types of innovations were defined: products, processes, business models, sources of supply and mergers and divestments. It is also important to distinguish innovations from ideas, because innovations are associated with a particular social activity related to commercialization. Thus, implementation of innovations is also a manifestation of entrepreneurship / entrepreneur's activity. Definitions of innovation evolved from purely Schumpeterian associating innovation with the activities of industrial enterprises to accentuating the social aspects. In fact, innovations in the modern sense do not have to have a physical form.

Due to the variety of definitions, numerous varied classification divisions of innovations can be found in the literature. Depending on the adopted criteria or purpose, the identified innovations can be assigned to different groups. In the course of technological development, various classifications of innovation appeared. The following table shows selected criteria allowing for the setting apart of different innovation types.

Table 23. Classification of innovations

Criteria	Types of innovation	Description
perspective of various disciplines of science and spheres of life	anthropocentric	related to various aspects of life
	technical	related to changes in technology
	biotic	related to the nature
	social	related to human relations
subject	product-oriented	the launch of a new or improved product
	process-oriented	change in production methods
	organizational	change in the functioning of organization
extent of the effects	strategic	include long-term projects having high socio-economic significance or related to the implementation of strategic objectives
	tactical	include ongoing changes in processes, products and organizations leading to improved efficiency

scale	radical	changes revolutionizing the production
	improving the production / incremental	are related to modernization
originality	pioneering	solutions that were not previously used
	adaptable (duplicating, imitative)	solutions used before, but beneficial in a given place and time
the degree of novelty	worldwide	new in the global scale
	countrywide or industrywide	constituting a new solution in the scale of a country or an industry
	enterprise-wide	constituting a new solution in the scale of an enterprise
process complexity	coupled	a result of the work of many people, teams or institutions
	isolated	a result of the work of a single individual, rationalizing operations
a change map	regular	not causing any sudden changes in the production area or market relations sphere but causing changes throughout an enterprise
	creating a niche	concerning amendments to the existing market relations -do not cause significant changes in the production area
	revolutionary	regarding changes in the production area, do not cause significant changes in market relations
	architectural	causing radical changes in both the production and the market
knowledge of the components and the system	incremental	related to the improvement of a product existing in the market by improving its components, without significant changes in the components themselves
	radical	related to significant changes in the components and their architecture
	modular	using the architecture of the components and availing of new ones to create a completely new design
	architectural	related to changes in system configuration; components

		remain the same
	product	related to changes in products / services
	process	related to changes in the methods of manufacturing or providing a product / service
4Ps of innovation	position	related to changes in the context in which the products / services are introduced
	paradigm	related to changes in mental models defining and formulating activities of the organization

Source: own based on [Zastempowski 2010, p. 55–71].

Another noteworthy classification is the one used by Eurostat and described in the Oslo Manual, where four basic types of innovations - presented in the table below - were distinguished. This classification follows the definition of innovation: "An innovation is the implementation of a new or significantly improved product (good or service), or process, a new marketing method, or a new organisational method in business practices, workplace organisation or external relations" [Oslo Manual, p. 46].

In the statistical research of innovation there also appears a concept of technological innovation, denoting the introduction of - at the scale of the enterprise as a minimum - a new or significantly improved product or process.

Table 24. Oslo innovation classification

Area of innovation implementation	Description	Example
process	introduction of a new or significantly improved production / supply method	implementation of new devices that automate the process of production; introduction of GPS localisation in transport services
product	introduction of a significantly improved product or service using the new knowledge / technology	the use of a new material, incorporating new software to improve functionality
organisation	implementation of a new method in the rules of the enterprise operation or its relationships with the environment	introduction of new rules aimed at improving learning and sharing / codification of knowledge in the enterprise
marketing	implementation of a new marketing method	changes in product design, a new distribution channel, a change in strategy

Source: own [based on *Oslo Manual*, p. 46–52]

Implementation of innovation may relate to one or more of its types but it is assumed that innovation is present if the solution in a given area is new, at least at the scale of the enterprise. Scientific, technical, organizational and financial efforts aimed at implementing innovation are at the heart of innovation activities of enterprises. Peter Drucker stressed that despite the difficulties and risks associated with innovation activities, they should be well organized and rational. It can therefore be assumed that one of the most important factors in the development of an enterprise is its ability to manage innovation activities.

In the literature, the concept of innovation often arises in the context of entrepreneurship. The reason for such connection is related to the fact that usually the essence of the innovation process is finding opportunities and ways of using them to achieve tangible benefits. Often technology is the factor that allows you to make radical choices. Innovative activity is related to actions of scientific, organizational, financial, technical and commercial nature. The nature of the changes (type of innovation) is often linked to a certain degree of risk, too. Thus, taking up innovative activity can be treated as a manifestation of entrepreneurship.

The implementation of the innovation process is influenced by various factors. Tidd and Bessant [Tidd, Bessant 2011, p. 107] claim that the most important ones include:

— sector;
— size of the enterprise;
— national systems for the promotion of innovation;
— life cycle;
— the degree of novelty;
— the role of external institutions.

If it is assumed that innovation (innovative activity) is a process, then the full and commonly accepted knowledge of the effects of such process and its internal workings are necessary.

With time and with the development of organization and management sciences, various models of innovativeness and innovation management are proposed. To the five generations of innovation models proposed by Rothwell [Rothwell 1992] at the beginning of the 1990s, another one has been added recently. These include [Marinova, Phillimore 2003]:

I generation – the "black box" model;
II generation – the linear models including models "pushed" by technology and "pulled" by the market;

III generation – interactive models, including coupled and integrated models;
IV generation – system models, including networks and national innovation systems;
V generation – evolutionary models;
VI generation – innovation environment models.
These models should also be supplemented with the general model proposed by Smith [Smith, 2006, p. 107]. It consists of two phases (research/development and commercialization) and seven consecutive stages (see Figure 10).

Although the steps are clearly separated in the model, the author concludes that in practice the boundaries between them may be blurred and the same steps can also penetrate each other or be executed in a different order.

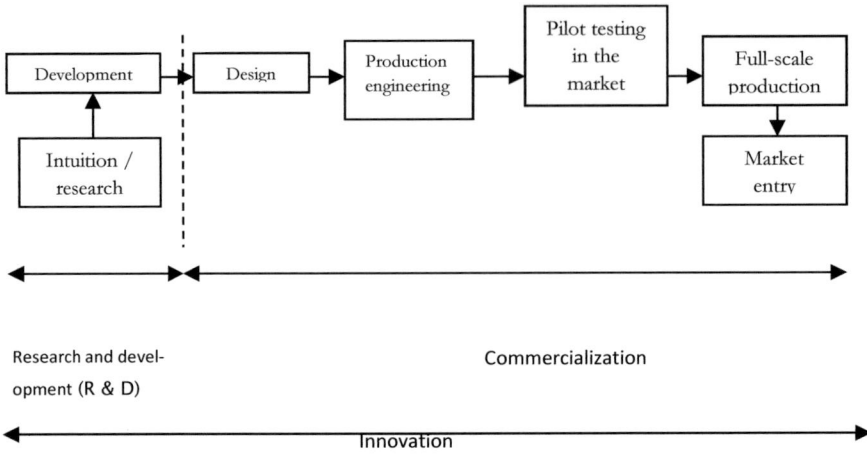

Figure 10. General model of innovation activity
Source:[Smith, p. 107].

The black box model assumes that the process of innovation is not important — only the input and output are essential. Thus, this model, combined with the reluctance of economists and other researchers to determine the relationship between science, technology and development, is the main reason for their failure to formulate appropriate policies to support innovation.

The linear models include two basic varieties: innovation pushed by science and pulled by the market. In demand and supply models the basic difference is related to the source of innovation (Figure 11 and 12).

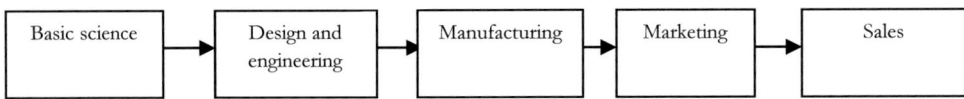

Figure 11. Technology-push model of innovation process
Source: [Rothwell 1994].

The model of innovation pushed by science was popular in the 1960s and is similar to the general model proposed by Smith and based on Schumpeter's concept.

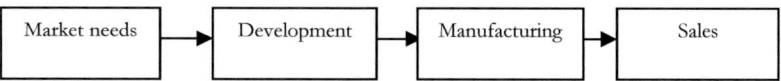

Figure 12. Market-pull model of innovation process
Source: [Rothwell 1994].

The demand model has gained popularity mainly due to the fact that innovative activity is associated in this case with a flexible response to market demands. The demand approach to innovation means also a partial transfer of initiative in the field of innovation to customers. Implementation of demand innovations often requires small and medium-sized enterprises to make changes in their functioning. [Baran, Ostrowska, Pander 2012, p. 27–28]

Due to the fact that individual actions in the innovation process need not and generally do not occur sequentially, the process itself and the sources of innovation are better reflected in the coupled (interactive) model, which takes into account the linkages between science, technology and production (see Figure 13). Innovation arises from the interaction between the market, the research and development base and the capacity of the organization.

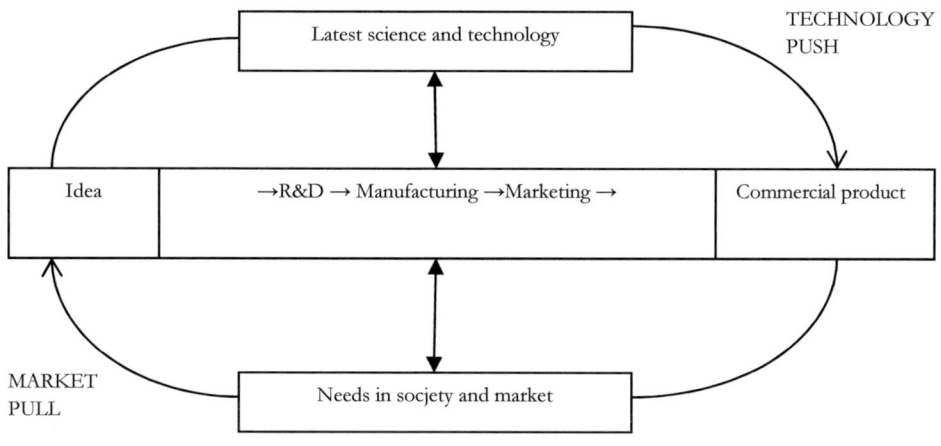

Figure 13. Interactive model of innovation process
Source: [Trott, p. 23].

The cyclic innovation model proposed by Berkhout [Berkhout 2006 in Ribiere, Tuggle 2010] emphasizes that the implementation of innovation is not a linear process but rather a result of cooperation and interaction of multiple specialists in different fields.

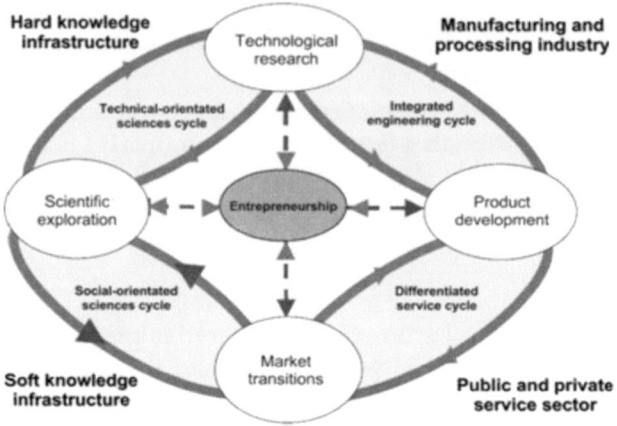

Figure 14. Cyclic innovation model
Source: [Berkhout et al. 2006 in Ribiere, Tuggle 2010].

The last, sixth generation of innovation models defines innovation as a creative combination of general knowledge and specific competencies. This concept helps to explain the successes of SMEs, which — with limited resources — pursue aggressive research and development strategies and use innovative technologies. This category includes the so-called open innovation, where the innovation process is based on the open source approach[18]. The enterprises often engage customers in adapting this approach to innovation. [see: Chesbrough 2003] The differences between the open and closed innovation approach are shown in the table below.

Table 25. The rules for creating closed and open innovations

Closed Innovation Principles	Open Innovation Principles
The smart people in our field work for us.	Not all of the smart people work for us, so we must find and tap into the knowledge and expertise of bright individuals outside our company.
To profit from R&D, we must discover, develop and ship it ourselves.	External R&D can create significant value; internal R&D is needed to claim some portion of that value.
If we discover it ourselves, we will get it to market first.	We don't have to originate the research in order to profit from it.
If we are the first to commercialize an innovation, we will win.	Building a better business model is better than getting to market first.

---

[18] The term is most commonly associated with software having publicly available source code.

If we create the most and best ideas in the industry, we will win.	If we make the best use of internal *and* external ideas, we will win.
We should control our intellectual property (IP) so that our competitors don't profit from our ideas.	We should profit from others' use of our IP, and we should buy others' IP whenever it advances **our own** business model.

Source:[Chesbrough 2003, p. 38].

In the literature — regardless of business model of innovation — sources of innovation are also considered important. The distinction between internal and external sources is most common. The internal sources include research and development facilities, qualifications of staff (creativity, lack of fear of change, speed of response to emerging opportunities and threats), as well as management (creating a climate and culture conducive to the implementation of innovation process). The external sources of innovation include the national (public information, the research and development sphere including universities, scientific institutions, research and development units and development centres) and international ones (the results of foreign research and development institutions, public information). Typically, the use of these sources is related to transfer of knowledge, exchange of staff, joint ventures or purchasing licenses, know-how or equipment. [see e.g. Zastempowski 2010, p. 71–77; *Oslo Manual* 2005, p. 72–88]

In recent years, the social innovations aroused interest of the theorists and practitioners. They are primarily a result of ongoing civilizational changes. Social innovation is defined as the introduction of new ideas in response to social needs and creating new relationships and areas of cooperation. Their main aim is improving the level and quality of life. Typically, these innovations are related to services. Social innovations are created in a process consisting of four basic steps [Guide to social innovation 2013, p. 6-9]:

— identification of unmet social needs,
— development of new solutions in response to these needs,
— evaluation of the effectiveness of the proposed solutions,
— scaling up of effective innovations.
The model of social innovation is shown in the figure below.

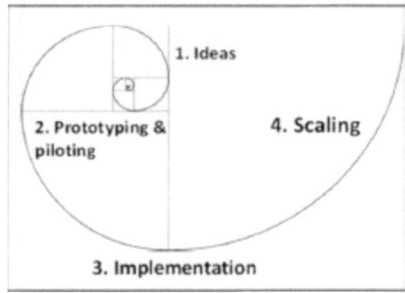

Figure 15. The spiral model of social innovation
Source: [Guide to social innovation 2013, p.9].

According to the Bureau of European Policy Advisors, social innovations can be seen from three perspectives [BEPA 2011, p. 36–40]:

— social demand – these are directed to vulnerable social groups;
— social challenges – these are directed to society as a whole;
— systemic changes – these are aimed at systemic changes (in attitudes, value system, strategy or policy).

The social innovations are not yet included in the classification proposed by the Oslo Manual. Social innovation can be seen in the context of the opportunities and challenges arising in connection with the following social trends:

— demography – migration and ageing of European societies;
— environment – climate change, water, energy;
— communication – digital society arising due to new IT solutions;
— poverty – poverty, including child poverty, social exclusion;
— health and well-being – inequalities in access to health services and care;
— ethics – fair trade and local production.

As also noted by Mulgan, Tucker, Sanders and Rushanara [Mulgan, Tucker, Sanders and Rushanara 2007], in the case of social innovations three key properties are important:

— they constitute an unprecedented combination of pre-existing elements;
— their implementation is associated with crossing organizational, domain-specific or sector boundaries;
— they allow for the creation of new relationships between those involved in their implementation, which often opens up new possibilities or initiates the creation of further innovations.

Murray, Caulier-Grice and Mulgan [Murray, Caulier-Grice, Mulgan 2010] mention six phases to enable the implementation of social innovation: prompts, inspirations and diagnoses; proposals and ideas; prototyping and pilots; sustaining, scaling and diffusion.

Guide to social innovation [Guide to social innovation 2013], on the other hand, highlights ten steps of social innovation implementation shown in the figure below — the key ones are:

1 – learn about social innovation,
4 – develop a smart specialization strategy and plan including social innovations,
6 – transition innovation platform,
7 – incubation trajectory specifically targeted at social innovation,
8 – social innovation cluster/ laboratory.

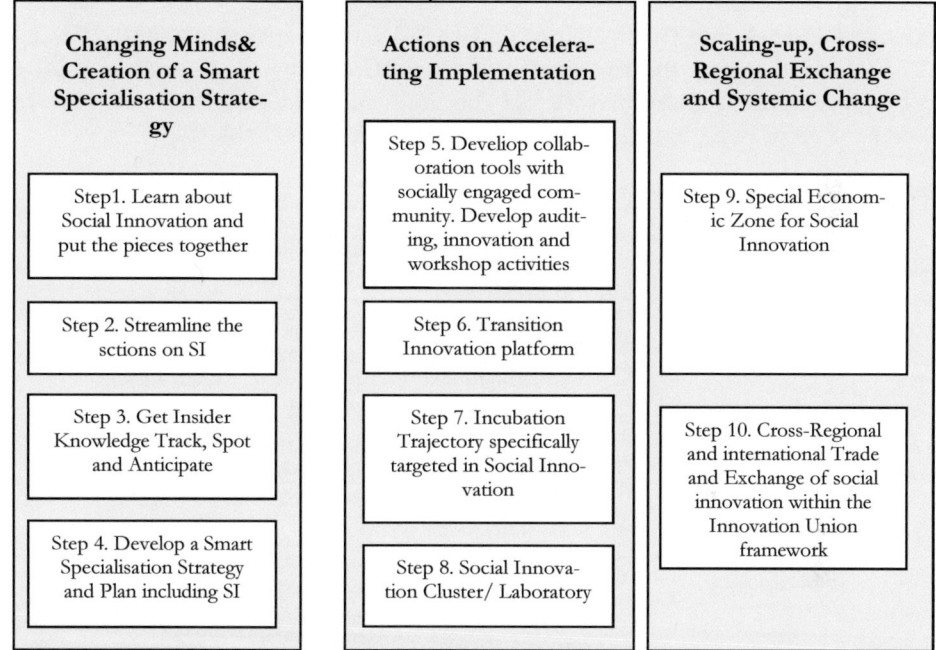

Figure 16. Practical steps to implement social innovation
Source: [Guide to social innovation 2013, p. 59].

Implementation of social innovation, like all ventures, is associated with high risk. This kind of innovations, however, requires a special commitment, perseverance as well as creating partnerships and trust in developing and then implementing new solutions.

The nature of the modern innovation process is well described by the qualities of innovation mentioned by Guinet [Guinet 1995 in Zastempowski 2010]:

— innovation only sometimes depends solely on technological knowledge;
— innovation is interactive and multidisciplinary;
— innovation is localized;
— innovation is a process of integration;
— innovation is a process of learning;
— innovation is a phenomenon having a social dimension;
— innovation is a process of creative destruction;
— innovation is costly and risky.

Kotler and Trias de Bes [Kotler, Trias de Bes 2013] draw attention to the diversity of tasks performed within the framework of innovative activities, as well as roles that can be performed by those involved in the innovation process. Each of these roles requires different skills, aptitudes and personality traits. (see Table 26)

Table 26. Key roles in the innovation process

Role	Description
Activators	People initiating the innovation process but not involved in its remaining phases.
Browsers	Experts in locating and providing information to other team members.
Creators	The individuals whose task is to create ideas related to new concepts and business opportunities; those seeking new solutions at different stages of the innovation process.
Developers	Individuals who shape ideas and translate them into ready solutions.
Executors	Individuals involved in the implementation of innovation in the organization and in the market.
Facilitators	Those approving expenditures and investments needed to implement the innovation process.

Source: own based on [Kotler, Trias de Bes 2013]

The innovation process is shaped by the interactions between these roles and may proceed differently in particular organizations.

3. 2. The enterprise innovation indicators

Innovation indicators are simply a set of tools and systems used in the evaluation of innovative capacity of an organization.

As noted by Kotler and Trias de Bes [Kotler, Trias de Bes 2013, p. 237–238] innovation indicators, being objective and quantitative metrics, can be used for mutual comparisons of enterprises within a branch, comparisons of several business units within an enterprise or assessing the increase of innovation capacity of a company / business unit in time.

Innovation measures may also gain a strategic dimension by being used in the process of communication (defining and communicating strategies), control (monitoring the implementation of activities related to innovation), learning (finding new opportunities by analysing the value of indicators) and providing assessments for innovation promotion systems [Kotler, Trias de Bes 2013, p. 238]. Kotler and Trais de Bes distinguish four groups of indicators: measuring innovation performance in economic terms, measuring the intensity of innovative activities within a department / unit / organization, measuring the effectiveness of innovation activities and investments in such activities and measuring the degree of dissemination of the culture conducive to the implementation of the innovation process of an organization [Kotler, Trias de Bes 2013, p. 239–246] (see Figure 17).

To assess the innovativeness of an organization, an appropriate combination of indicators needs to be selected, as monitoring all of them can prove very costly and time-consuming. One can therefore choose indicators that complement or reflect goals and strategy of an organization. Another criterion for the selection of indicators is the specificity of industry and the identification of key success factors.

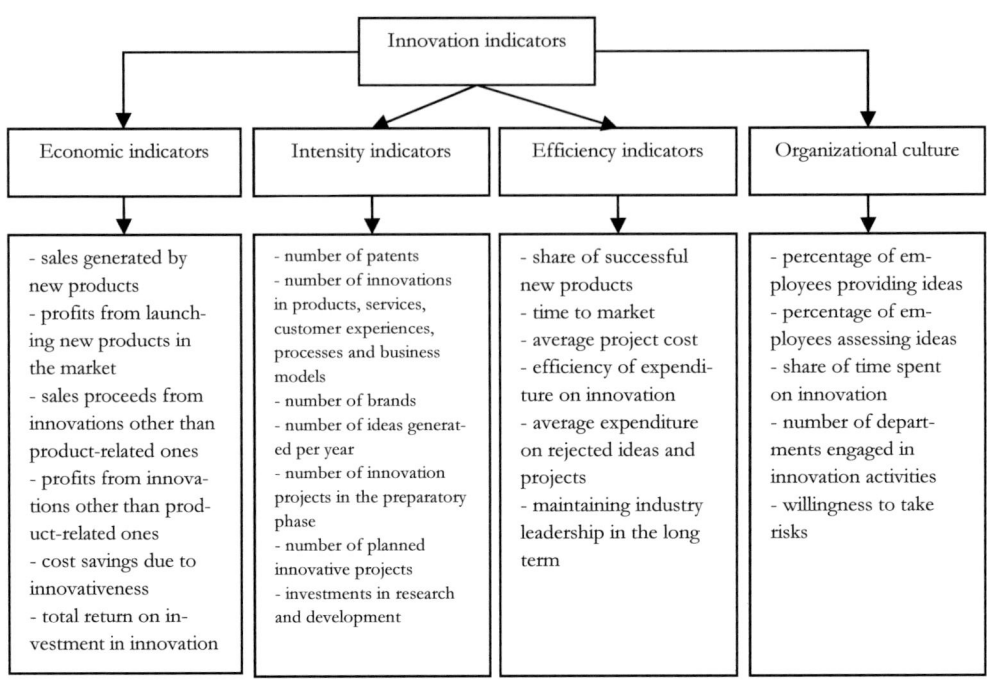

Figure 17. Indicators of enterprise innovation
Source: own based on [Kotler, Trias de Bes 2013, p. 239-246].

In the European Union annual reports evaluating the innovativeness of European countries, as well as worldwide innovation leaders, have been prepared for more than a decade. Statistical data related to various manifestations of innovative activity are collected in accordance with the methodology described in the Oslo Manual.

The most known are the reports prepared by Eurostat (Innovation Union Scoreboard — former European Innovation Scoreboard or European Innovation Progress Report) and OECD (Science, Technology and Industry Scoreboard).

In the newest Innovation Union Scoreboard report the data concerning three areas listed in the Table 27 are completed and analysed.

The indicators presented are grouped into three categories relating to inputs, processes and outputs. A similar approach is proposed by Kotler and Trias de Bes [Kotler, Trias de Bes 2013, p. 248–250]

Table 27. Types and dimensions of innovation drivers

Type	Dimensions	Indicators
ENABLERS	Human resources	New doctoral graduates
		Population with completed tertiary education
		Youth with upper secondary level education
	Open, excellent and attractive research systems	International scientific co-publications
		Scientific publications among top 10% most cited
		Non-EU doctorate students
	Finance and support	Public R&D expenditure
		Venture capital
FIRM ACTIVITIES	Firm investments	Business R&D expenditure
		Non-R&D innovation expenditure
	Linkages & entrepreneurship	SMEs innovating in-house
		Innovative SMEs collaborating with others
		Public-private co-publications
	Intellectual Assets	PCT patent applications
		PCT patent applications in societal challenges
		Community trademarks
		Community designs
OUTPUTS	Innovators	SMEs introducing product or process innovations
		SMEs introducing marketing/organisational innovations
	Economic effects	Employment in knowledge-intensive activities
		Medium and high-tech product exports
		Knowledge-intensive services exports
		Sales of new to market and new to firm innovations
		Licence and patent revenues from abroad

Source: own based on Eurostat.

In the OECD reports, the aspect of innovation is seen as one of the constituents of development of science and technology. The indicators presented in these studies relate primarily to the number of patents or spending on research and development. The are mainly used in knowledge-intensive industries (such as biotechnology or nanotechnology).

The methodology used by Eurostat to measure the level of innovation did not always reflect the phenomena occurring in this area in the European Union well. In September 2013, the European Commission, at the request of EU leaders, introduced an innovation index that allows for comparing national innovation strategies. It complements two other indicators of innovation that had been calculated for over 10 years: IUS (Innovation Union Scoreboard) and SII (Summary Innovation Index). The new index is based on four components selected for their relevance for policy: technological innovation measured by the number of patents, the share of employed in sectors requiring specialized knowledge, competitiveness of goods and services requiring specialized knowledge and the level of employment in the fast-growing innovative enterprises in innovative industries. The average value of this indicator for the EU in 2010 was 100 — it was determined based on the IUS 2013 indicator before the accession of Croatia to the EU. Countries that exploited the opportunities offered by innovation best were: Sweden, Germany, Ireland and Luxembourg. [Communication from the Commision 2014, COM (2013) 624]

While the reports prepared by Eurostat and the OECD relate to selected countries, the reports produced since 2007 by the WIPO (World Intellectual Property Organisation) in collaboration with Johnson Cornell University and INSEAD (The Business School for the World) cover a ranking of all countries. The Global Innovation Index is determined on the basis of the Innovation Efficiency Ratio. The structure of the indicator is shown in the figure below.

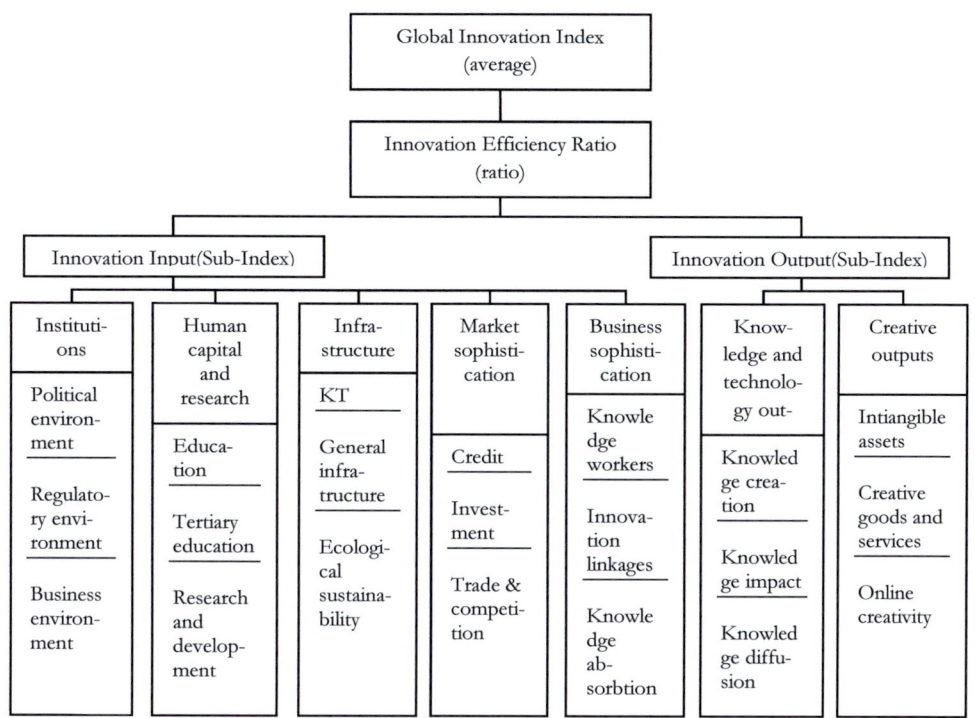

Figure 18. Global Innovation Index' structure.
Source: [GII 2013, p. 6].

Another noteworthy model is the Management Innovation Index (MIX), developed by the Australian consulting firm The Creative Leadership Forum Learning Centre Pty Ltd. This model has four axes corresponding to particular areas of innovation management: strategy, organization, management practices, attitudes of employees and organizational culture/work environment [http://www.managementinnovation.net/?page_id=6].

3. 3. Innovative enterprises in Europe and the BSR countries

The traditional European leaders of innovativeness are Sweden, Denmark, Germany and Finland. Sweden once again is the leader in innovation in the Eurostat report.

The largest increase of innovation indicators in the IUS 2013 report can be observed in other countries of the Baltic Sea Region: Estonia, Lithuania and Latvia. In contrast, Poland fared worse in the ranking and was placed in the weakest group of countries in terms of innovation.

The most frequently cited barriers to innovation include: lack of financial resources (both internal and external), high innovation costs, uncertain demand / lack of demand for innovation, market cornered by the competitors, problems in finding a partner for cooperation, lack of qualified personnel, lack of need because of previous experiences, as well as the lack of knowledge about the technology or market. Some of these barriers can be classified as internal, whereas the remaining ones - as external. Abolition or reduction of the internal barriers importance depends directly on the enterprise's willingness to take innovative activities. In fact, these barriers are often indicated in a slightly exaggerated way.

The Summary Innovation Index (SII) is a synthetic measure, built on the basis of the indicators listed in Table III.3. However, one should not jump to conclusions based on observations of the absolute value of this indicator, as the methodology of its calculation was changed in 2007.

As can be seen (table III.6), the analysis of the SII over 9 years allows for noticing some trends: in the case of Sweden, Denmark, Finland and Germany - the European innovation leaders - the index reached levels significantly higher than the European average; in the case of Estonia, the SII fluctuated slightly below the European average; by contrast, in Lithuania and Poland the innovation index remained more or less at the same level, constituting about a half of the European average. The last place in the BSR countries innovation ranking is taken by Latvia.

Table 28. Summary Innovation Index

Country/ year	2004	2005	2006	2007	2008	2009	2010	2011	2012
EU	0.429	0.431	0.447	0.446	0.504	0.516	0.532	0.531	0.544
DK	0.566	0.572	0.605	0.602	0.643	0.66	0.969	0.696	0.718
EE	0.413	0.409	0.421	0.443	0.415	0.458	0.46	0.484	0.5
FI	0.551	0.546	0.541	0.585	0.657	0.673	0.675	0.681	0.681
LT	0.264	0.273	0.287	0.294	0.244	0.248	0.255	0.271	0.28
LV	0.194	0.204	0.215	0.239	0.188	0.206	0.216	0.225	0.225
DE	0,538	0.543	0.548	0.569	0.677	0.944	0.71	0.705	0.72
PL	0.264	0.272	0.282	0.293	0.268	0.278	0.273	0.283	0.27

SE	0.607	0.61	0.637	0.63	0.725	0.731	0.733	0.735	0.747

Source: own elaboration based on Eurostat data.

The effects of innovation activity can be assessed by the share of enterprises in the implementation of product, process or organizational innovations.

The analysis of indicators related to the number of process or product innovations implemented in the countries of the Baltic Sea Region provides information on trends in these states. It may be noted that in Germany, Estonia, Finland, Sweden and Denmark the share of small and medium-sized enterprises implementing process or product innovations is higher than the European average. In contrast, Latvia, Lithuania and Poland SMEs are the least active in this area (see Table 29).

Table 29. SMEs introducing product or process innovations [%]

Country/ year	2008	2009	2010	2011	2012
EU	33.7	33.7	34.18	34.18	34.44
DK	35.7	35.7	37.63	37.63	41.6
EE	45.8	45.8	43.92	43.92	45.56
FI	44.7	44.7	41.83	41.83	44.75
LT	19.7	19.7	21.93	21.93	21.39
LV	14.4	14.4	17.22	17.22	15.78
DE	52.8	52.8	53.61	53.61	57.0
PL	20.4	20.4	17.55	17.55	14.36
SE	40.7	40.7	40.59	40.59	47.38

Source: own elaboration based on Eurostat data.

The innovative activity of enterprises is also accounted for by the number of organizational or marketing innovations. Due to gaps in statistical data it is difficult to draw firm conclusions, however. It can be noticed, though, that in the recent years - despite the fact that the percentage of enterprises at EU level has been staying approximately the same - the percentage of companies implementing innovations of this type in the Baltic countries has decreased.

Table 30. SMEs introducing marketing or organizational innovations [%]

Country/ year	2004	2005	2006	2007	2008	2009	2010	2011	2012
EU	-	-	-	-	33.7	33.7	34.18	34.18	34.44
DK	26	26	57.1	57.1	45.4	45.4	40.02	40.02	42.64
EE	53	52.5	39.2	39.2	48.4	48.4	34.1	34.1	35.99
FI	47	47	47	-	-	-	31.49	31.49	38.89
LT	31	30.7	23.6	23.6	28.5	28.5	21.39	21.39	26.39
LV	36	35.7	35.7	-	-	-	13.95	13.95	22.68
DE	65	65	53.2	53.2	68.1	68.1	68.18	62.63	60.55
PL	-	-	19.3	19.3	29.1	29.1	18.65	18.65	19.95
SE	44	44	44	-	-	-	36.73	36.73	42.15

Source: own elaboration based on Eurostat data.

The analysis of statistical data allows also for noting that the countries which spend more money on research and development and have a well-functioning system of boosting innovation achieve better results.

In the analysed period, an increase in spending on research and development in the public sector can be observed, although it still remains at a very low level. (see Table 31) For the assessment of innovative activity of enterprises, on the other hand, their participation in expenditure on research and development work is important (see Table 32). It can be noted that the enterprises from the countries being the innovation leaders are more aware of the need to invest their own resources in research and development. However, the percentage of enterprises incurring expenditure in this area does not exceed 4%.

Table 31. R&D expenditures in the public sector [%of GDP]

Country/ year	2004	2005	2006	2007	2008	2009	2010	2011	2012
EU	0.67	0.69	0.65	0.65	0.65	0.67	0.75	0.76	0.75
DK	0.77	0.8	0.76	0.76	0.88	0.81	0.99	0.96	0.99
EE	0.55	0.53	0.5	0.5	0.58	0.71	0.76	0.79	0.87
FI	1.04	1.03	0.99	0.99	0.94	0.94	1.11	1.1	1.09
LT	0.54	0.54	0.61	0.61	0.58	0.62	0.64	0.56	0.68
LV	0.25	0.25	0.34	0.34	0.42	0.46	0.29	0.38	0.5
DE	0.77	0.77	0.76	0.76	0.76	0.79	0.9	0.92	0.94
PL	0.46	0.43	0.39	0.39	0.38	0.41	0.41	0.53	0.53
SE	0.95	1.02	0.92	0.92	0.99	0.97	1.06	1.07	1.03

Source: own elaboration based on Eurostat data.

Table 32. R&D expenditures in the business sector [%of GDP]

Country/ year	2004	2005	2006	2007	2008	2009	2010	2011	2012
EU	1.27	1.26	1.2	1.17	1.17	1.21	1.25	1.23	1.27
DK	1.75	1.84	1.67	1.67	1.65	1.91	2.02	2.08	2.09
EE	0.22	0.28	0.42	0.42	0.54	0.56	0.64	0.81	1.49
FI	2.37	2.45	2.92	2.46	2.51	2.76	2.83	2.35	2.34
LT	0.14	0.14	0.16	0.16	0.23	0.19	0.2	0.56	0.24
LV	0.17	0.14	0.23	0.23	0.21	0.15	0.17	0.38	0.19
DE	1.73	1.75	1.76	1.76	1.77	1.84	1.92	1.9	1.9
PL	0.13	0.16	0.18	0.18	0.18	0.19	0.18	0.2	0.23
SE	3.32	2.93	2.46	2.92	2.64	2.78	2.54	2.35	2.34

Source: own elaboration based on Eurostat data.

The level of enterprise innovation potential is also affected by the quality and qualifications of staff, as well as by cooperating with other units within the framework of the innovative activities.

As can be seen in the Baltic Sea Region countries, the research and development personnel constitutes — at best — about 3% of total number of employees. This ratio is higher in the Nordic countries. A growing trend in this area of employment has also been observed in all Baltic Sea Region countries apart from Poland (see Table 33).

Table 33. Total R&D personnel and researchers [% of total labour force and total employment]

Country/ year	2003	2005	2007	2009	2011
EU	1.33	1.38	1.46	1.53	1.66
DK	2.11	2.33	2.35	2.85	2.92
EE	1.67	1.64	1.74	1.86	1.97
FI	1.15	1.2	1.35	1.43	1.46
LT	0.72	0.84	0.93	0.78	0.98
LV	0.89	1.02	1.16	1.14	1.51
DE	0.75	0.72	0.72	0.7	0.78
PL	2.88	2.95	2.97	2.97	3.01
SE	2.34	2.5	2.39	2.35	2.49

Source: own elaboration based on Eurostat data.

In contrast, in the coming years the employment in knowledge-intensive sectors will be rather falling in all countries of the Baltic Sea Region, as well as on average in the European Union. This is confirmed by the data in Table 34.

Table 34. Employment in knowledge-intensive activities [% of total labour force and total employment]

Country/ year	2003	2005	2007	2009	2011
EU	1.33	1.38	1.46	1.53	1.66
DK	2.11	2.33	2.35	2.85	2.92
EE	1.67	1.64	1.74	1.86	1.97
FI	1.15	1.2	1.35	1.43	1.46
LT	0.72	0.84	0.93	0.78	0.98
LV	0.89	1.02	1.16	1.14	1.51
DE	0.75	0.72	0.72	0.7	0.78
PL	2.88	2.95	2.97	2.97	3.01
SE	2.34	2.5	2.39	2.35	2.49

Source: own elaboration based on Eurostat data.

The enterprises from the Nordic countries cooperate within the framework of the innovation process most frequently. In Sweden, Finland, Denmark and Estonia cooperation within the framework of innovative activity is undertaken more frequently in comparison to the European Union average. On the other hand, in Poland, Latvia and Lithuania, this ratio is lower than the EU average.

Table 35. Innovative SMEs collaborating with others [%]

Country/ year	2004	2005	2006	2007	2008	2009	2010	2011	2012
EU	7.1	8.6	8.4	9.1	9.5	9.5	11.16	11.16	11.69
DK	15.8	16.6	20.8	20.8	14.9	14.9	22.68	22.23	15.46
EE	11.3	11.3	16	16	18.1	18.1	22.29	22.23	18.52
FI	20	18.6	17.3	17.3	27.5	27.5	15.3	15.3	16.5
LT	12.3	12.3	14.8	14.8	10.3	10.3	8.03	8.03	8.76
LV	4	6.2	6.1	6.1	5.6	5.6	3.29	3.29	4.19
DE	9.2	9.2	8.6	8.6	9	9	8.95	8.95	14.01
PL	5	8.2	9.1	9.1	9.3	9.3	6.4	6.4	4.15
SE	13.4	13.4	20	20	16.6	16.6	16.51	16.51	17.47

Source: own elaboration based on Eurostat data.

In turn, according to the latest Global Innovation Index [Dutta, Lanvin 2013] report, the highest level of the index among the countries of the Baltic Sea Region was achieved by Sweden, and the worst one by Poland (see Figure 19).

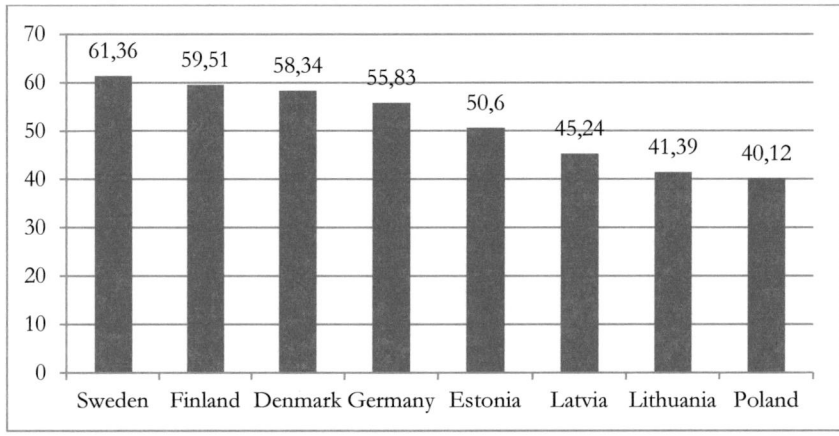

Figure 19. Global Innovation Index 2013 (max. score 100)
Source: own elaboration based on [Dutta, Lanvin 2013].

Despite such unfavourable total assessment of Poland, the enterprise and state budget spending on research and development during the recent crisis was showing a rising trend. [Dutta, Lanvin 2013, p. 4]

It has been stated that the activities related to the implementation of economic policy in many countries are still associated with the stimulation of economic growth. The innovative strategies should provide the basis for improving productivity and increasing the number of jobs. The sources for new innovations can be found in areas such as education, environment, energy, information technology and transport. It is therefore necessary to determine priority areas to ensure stable growth, but also to resolve the economic, social and environmental challenges facing the modern economy. It has to be remembered that failing to invest in research and development now could result in lowering the future innovation potential, too.

It is emphasized that innovation today is global in nature, although in terms of scientific research concentration can be observed in certain areas — new centres of expertise are created in Europe and Asia.

Innovation research highlights the regional and local dimension of innovation and innovation support systems. It has also been found that the linear model of the innovation process, popular since the 1990s, is not working nowadays. It focused on providing the infrastructure for research and development, financial support and technology transfer but it did not take into account the absorption capacity of the enterprises or the need for specific innovation or support in less developed regions. The factors such as the specificity of management and organizational deficit in small and medium-sized enterprises were also omitted. The analysis and research (e.g. of strengths and weaknesses of local industry or access to finance or markets) allowed for the selection of more efficient regions and indicating the possibilities of creating specific clusters [Dutta, Lanvin 2013].

The Global Innovation Index takes into account the holistic perception of innovation. It consists of two sub-indicators: innovation input sub-index and innovation output sub-index. The input stream consists of five elements: institutions, human capital and research, infrastructure, market sophistication and business sophistication. In total, 84 different indicators are researched. The output elements are knowledge, technology and creative outputs. The final value of the GII ratio is achieved by comparing the outputs with the inputs [Dutta, Lanvin 2013, p. 6–8].

3.4. European innovation policy – assumptions and current effects

According to the strategy of creating innovative Europe developed by independent experts, the need for intensification of activities in several areas was indicated [Aho 2006]. First of all, it is necessary to develop an appropriate strategy to create a European market for stimulating and supporting innovative activity. This is related to the development of a system of incentives for enterprises to intensify research and development, initiate cooperation in this field with research and development institutions or use new technological solutions. It is also necessary to create a market for innovative products and services. Activities in this area relate primarily to the creation of the so-called climate for innovation, which includes relevant regulations, public support, intellectual capital and innovation culture. Research and development in turn requires providing appropriate facilities. Particular attention should be paid to increasing the productivity of research and development sector. As a basis for innovation-driven success the structural mobility in three main areas is indicated: labour, finance, organization and knowledge. It is also necessary to achieve agreement on research and innovation between politicians, business and social leaders.

As stated in the assessment of the periodic implementation of innovation strategies in OECD countries [OECD 2009], innovation will be the key to return to the path of sustainable growth after overcoming the crisis. The new, global dimension of innovation should, however, be taken into account, so that the strategy actually allows countries for appropriate transformation and availing of the potential of innovation to promote economic development. Innovation is presented in the report as the key factor for growth, creating new knowledge for value generation. The importance of intangible assets and the need to find a way to measure them is also stressed. Nowadays, innovation should respond to global challenges, so it is necessary to address them properly. Attention was also paid to the growing importance of non-technological, organizational and social innovation. The innovative activity has never been easy and risk-free but now is becoming more and more complex. It is therefore necessary to focus on those elements that are part of the competitive advantage (defining specialization) and to cooperate within the framework of the innovation process with other partners. The open innovation model called earlier in this chapter can be used here. Another important aspect is the creation of a platform to support the generation and transfer of knowledge. The key role in creating the demand for and supply of innovation is to be played by the entrepreneurs.

In the OECD report [OECD 2011b] it is noted that the policy of shaping demand for innovation can be used both to achieve a higher rate of innovation and to increase the efficiency of public spending through innovation in the areas of intense social demand. The success of such a policy is dependent on a number of strategic factors, i.a. determining whether the actions taken are commercially effective or improve social welfare, defining the appropriate sectoral orientation of innovation, management and coordination of policy within the public sector, as well as establishing common goals for all stakeholders (including companies). The case studies conducted within the research made it possible to formulate recommendations for policy of steering the demand for innovation:

— assessment of the legitimacy of a policy of intervention in the area of innovation, as well the possibility of creating such policy — the instruments of such policy may result in increased costs for enterprises but can also open up new business opportunities;

— considering the sector and market issues — some instruments will stimulate the emergence of innovations, while others may support the processes of diffusion;
— the scale and duration of the intervention policy should depend on the risk, the significant activities conducted by market players or the technological constraints;
— the policy of increasing demand for innovation must be coupled with the relevant instruments on the supply side;
— it is possible to increase the demand for innovation by increasing the innovation capacity of the public sector — this may help to meet the social and global challenges;
— application of incentives and regulations can promote the innovativeness of public procurement in accordance with the principles of transparency, accountability and good governance;
— to encourage the public administration to work towards innovation, tools can be used on both the demand and the supply side of innovation — however, such promotion of innovativeness is most commonly associated with carrying out administrative reforms and increasing the competencies of human resources;
— the means of increasing user involvement in the development and diffusion of innovative solutions include proper education policy and consumer protection.

The comparative analysis of selected countries related to the field of business innovation support policies conducted by the OECD in 2011 [OECD 2011a] allowed for identifying the key instruments that countries can use in this area. They include co-financing of certain research and development activities and other innovation-related activity, or tax preferences for companies performing research and development. In any case, the particular circumstances of a country should of course be considered — therefore, the innovation support policy will be a different combination of instruments, measures and specific solutions. The report presents also good practices related to co-financing research and development activities or the use of tax credits in Denmark, Britain, the Netherlands and Finland. Attention has also been drawn to the important role of the public sector in the implementation of policies of stimulating demand for innovation.

The reports prepared by the World Intellectual Property Organisation [Gurry, Fink et al. 2011, 2012, 2013] emphasized the special role of intellectual capital in the creation and transfer of knowledge. Indicators related to research and development activities and outcomes are primarily examined (patents, trademarks, brands). The internationalization and the increasing openness of innovation processes have also been noted.

The direction outlined for Europe in the Aho report is basically maintained. This is confirmed by further initiatives and strategies developed by the European Commission or on its behalf[19] [see also Kincsö and Edler 2011, European Commission 2010b].

Europe 2020 Strategy sets out three priorities [European Commission 2010a, 2010b]:

1. smart growth - related to the development of an economy based on knowledge and innovation;
2. sustainable development - based on promoting resource-efficient economies which take into account environmental requirements, while being more competitive than others;
3. inclusive growth - promoting measures to increase employment, ensuring social and territorial cohesion.

The European Commission has also presented seven flagship projects enabling the implementation of individual priorities and detailed objectives associated with them [see more: European Commission 2010a]:

— Innovation Union;
— Youth on the Move;
— Digital Agenda for Europe;
— Resource Efficient Europe;
— Industrial policy for the globalization era;
— Agenda for new skills and jobs;
— The European Platform against Poverty.

The Commission's report for the European Parliament [European Commission 2013] stated that the economic recovery in 2010 was greater in countries which have invested in research and development, such as Sweden, Finland and Germany. Public and private investment in research and development grew before the start of the economic crisis. Following the start of the crisis, overall spending on research and development increased from 1.85% of GDP in 2007 to 2.03% in 2011, however in eleven EU countries public investment grew more slowly than GDP (within the BSR countries in Latvia and Lithuania). In many countries reforms aimed at increasing the efficiency of research and innovation systems in accordance with the objectives of the European Research Area have also been initiated. Upcoming are also new laws concerning innovation, as well as national strategies of development and innovation. In many Member States solutions aimed at increasing the autonomy of universities related to

---

[19] e.g. creating European Innovative Partnership or preparing the handbook on Public Procurement for Innovation [http://ec.europa.eu/research/innovation-union/index_en.cfm?pg=eip]

cooperation with the private sector or the commercialization of knowledge are prepared or implemented. Public-private cooperation and internationalization of enterprises are the basis for cluster policies implemented in recent years in many EU countries. The relationship between the level of employment and the economic impact of innovation has also been noted, which justifies paying attention to the fast growing knowledge-based markets, where the potential to create new jobs is greater (see Figure 20). Only people with skills tailored to the needs of the labour market will find employment, which implies the need for change in the education system. The report also highlights the necessity of shaping the demand for innovative products and services.

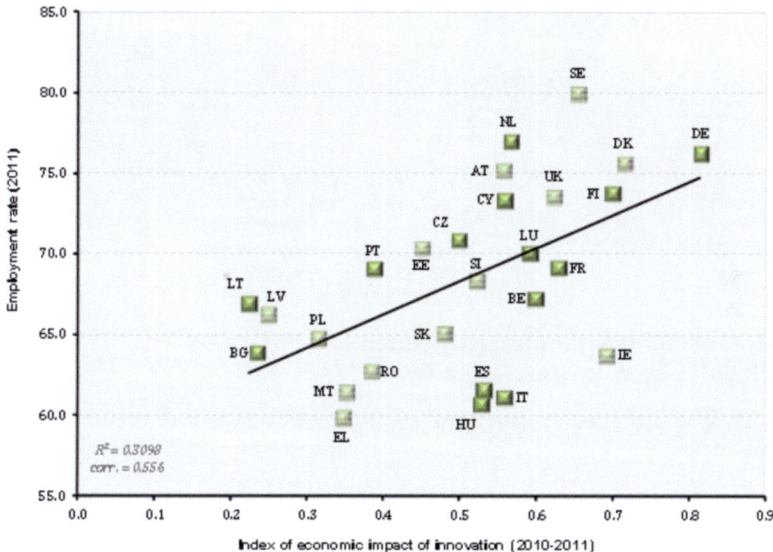

Figure 20. Correlation between economic impact of innovation and employment
Source: [European Commission 2013].

The reports on the level of innovation of individual countries or regions show that differences between countries and regions are still persisting. Better results are achieved by regions in the most innovative countries. These regional differences confirm the need to adapt innovation policies to the achievements of regions (see Figure 21). This approach is to be promoted within the framework of the 2014–2020 cohesion policy (see: http://ec.europa.eu/regional_policy/what/future/index_en.cfm).

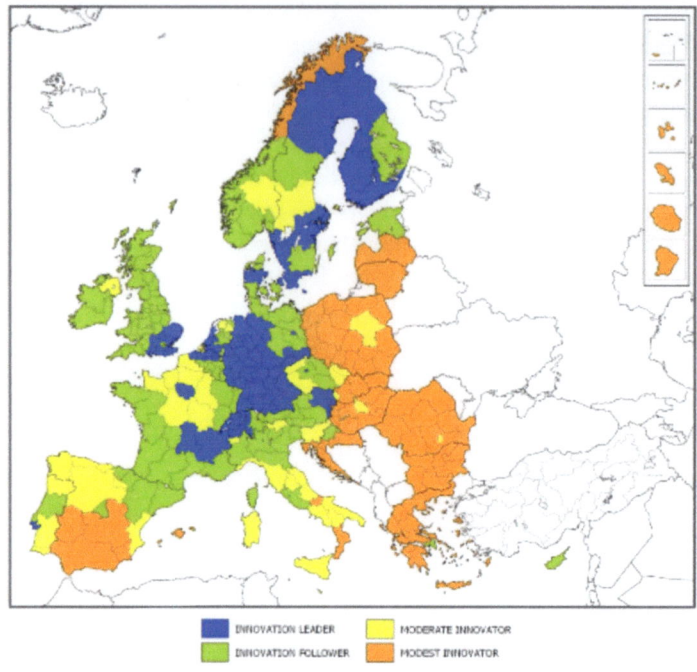

Figure 21. Innovation performance by region
Source: [Hollader, Leon, Roman 2012, p. 6].

The report also includes recommendations related to the concentration of further actions on:

— acceleration of structural changes — diversification of new sectorso, supporting fast developing innovative companies;
— reducing regional differences in innovation through smart specialization and co-ordination of the Horizon 2020 programme and structural funds;
— creating the conditions for the functioning of innovative enterprises, also within the framework of cluster initiatives;
— looking for ways to increase the public sector innovativeness;
— developing a strategy favouring an open approach to the process of innovation and knowledge transfer;
— protecting intellectual property;
— promoting innovation in retail trade, or
— combining new technologies and services with new business models.

References

1. Aho E. (ed.), *Creating an innovative Europe. Independent Expert Group on R&D and Innovation appointed following the Hampton Court Summit and chaired by Mr. Esko Aho*, European Commission, Luxembourg 2006
2. Baran M., Ostrowska A., Pander W., *Innowacje popytowe, czyli jak się tworzy współczesne innowacje*, Polska Agencja Rozwoju Przedsiębiorczości, Warszawa 2012
3. Chesbrough, Henry W. (2003), The Era of Open Innovation,Sloan Management Review, 44, 3 (Spring): 35-41
4. Cohension policy 2014-2020 [http://ec.europa.eu/regional_policy/ what/future/index_en.cfm, access 6-12-2013]
5. Communication from the Commission to the European Parliament, The Council, The European Economic and Social Committee and the Committee of the Regions: *Measuring innovation output in Europe: towards a new indicator*, Brussels, 13.9.2013, COM(2013) 624 final
6. Dutta S., Lanvin B. (2013), *The Global Innovation Index 2013. The Local Dynamics of Innovation*, Cornell Univeristy, INSEAD and WIPO, Geneva
7. Edler J. and Georghiou L. (2007), *Public procurement and innovation- Resurrecting the demand side*, Elsevier, Volume 36, Issue 7, September 2007, Pages 949–963
8. European Commission (2010a). Communication, *Europe 2020 A strategy for smart, sustainable and inclusive growth*, COM(2010) 2020 final, 3.3.2010
9. European Commission (2010b). Communication, *Europe 2020 Flagship Initiative Innovation Union*, COM(2010) 546 final, 6.10.2010
10. European Commission (2011), *Emproving people, driving change. Social Innovation in European Union*, BEPA, European Commission, Luxembourg
11. European Commission (2013). Communication, *State of the Innovation Union 2012 – Accelerating change*, COM(2013) 149 final, Brussels, 21.3.2013
12. European Innovation Partnership [http://ec.europa.eu/research/innovation-union/index_en.cfm?pg=eip, access 6-12-2013]
13. Guinet J. (1995), National System for Financing Innovation, OECD, Paris
14. Gurry F., Fink C. at all (2011), *World Intelellectual Property Report 2011*, World Innelectual Property Organisation [http://www.wipo.int/export/sites/www/ freepublications/en/intproperty/944/wipo_pub_944_2011.pdf, access 6-12-2013]
15. Gurry F., Fink C. at all (2012), *World Intelellectual Property Indicators 2012*, World Innelectual Property Organisation [http://www.wipo.int/export/sites/www/ freepublications/en/intproperty/941/wipo_pub_941_2012.pdf, access 6-12-2013]
16. Gurry F., Fink C. at all (2013), *World Intelellectual Property Report 2013. Brands-reputation and Image in the Global Marketplace* , World Innelectual Property Organisation [http://www.wipo.int/export/sites/www/freepublications/en/intproperty /944/wipo_pub_944_2013.pdf, access 6-12-2013]

17. Holladers H., Leon L.R., Roman L. (2012), *Regional Innovation Scoreboard 2012*, European Union, Luxembourg
18. Kincsö I. and Edler J. (2011), *Trends and Challenges in Demand-Side Innovation Policies in Europe*, Technopolis [http://ec.europa.eu/enterprise/newsroom/cf/_getdocument.cfm?doc_id=7011, access 2-12-2013]
19. Marinova D., Phillimore J., *Models of Innovation*, [in] Shavanina L.V. (ed.): The International Handbook of Innovation, Elseviere Science Ltd. 2003, ss. 44-53
20. Mulgan G., Tucker S, Rushanara, Sanders B. (2007), *Social Innovation. What it is, why it matters and how it can be accelerated*, Skoll Centre for Social Entrepreneurship, working paper
21. Murray R., Caulier-Grice J., Mulgan G.: *The open book of social innovation*, The Young Foundation, March 2010
22. OECD (2011 a), *Business Innovation Policies. Selcted country comparison*, OECD Publishing, Paryż [http://dx.doi.org/10.1787/9789264115668-en , access 29-11-2013]
23. OECD (2011 b), *Demand-side Innovation Policies*, OECD Publishing, Paryż [http://dx.doi.org/10.1787/9789264098886-en , access 29-11-2013]
24. OECD and European Communities (2005), Oslo Manual. Guidelines for collecting and interpreting innovation data. 3rd Edition, OECD Publishing, Paryż
25. OECD (2013), *OECD Science, Technology and Industry Scoreboard 2013: Innovation for Growth*, OECD Publishing, Paryż
26. Ribiere V. M., Tuggle F. D., *Fostering innovation with KM 2.0*, VINE, Vol. 40 Issue 1, (2010) pp.90 – 101
27. Rothwell R., *Towards the Fifth-generationInnovation Process*, International Marketing Review,Vol. 11 No. 1, 1994, pp. 7-31
28. Rothwell R.: *Successful industrial innovation: Critical success tactors for the 1990s*, "R&D Management", nr 22(3) 1992, s. 221-239
29. Schumpeter J.A. (1934) *The Theory of Economic Development*, Cambridge, Mass: Harvard University Press
30. Smith D. (2006), Exploring Innovation, The MacGraw-Hill Companies, New York
31. Tidd J., Bessant J.: *Zarządzanie innowacjami. Integracja zmian technologicznych, rynkowych i organizacyjnych*, Oficyna Wolters Kluwers business, Warszawa 2011
32. TrendChart mini country reports (2011) [http://ec.europa.eu/enterprise/policies/innovation/policy/innovation-scoreboard/country-reports_en.htm, access 6-12-2013]
33. Trott P., *Innovation Management and New Product Development*, Prentice Hall, 2005
34. Zastempowski M. (2010), *Uwarunkowania potencjału innowacyjnego polskich małych i średnich przedsiębiorstw*, Wydawnictwo Naukowe Uniwersytetu Mikołaja Kopernika, Toruń

Chapter IV The ageing population — a challenge at the- macro- and microeconomic level

4.1. The scale and pace of ageing in Europe

The ageing of the population consists in changing the regime of population reproduction (recreating its level and structure) from traditional (with high rates of deaths and births) to modern (with a low rate of deaths and births). In Europe, it started 100–150 years ago (depending on the country). As a result of declining birth rates and lengthening life expectancy, currently in all European countries there is an increase in the number and proportion of older individuals in the general population, i.e. the process of ageing is progressing [Racław, Rosochacka-Gmitrzak 2012].

This does not mean, however, that the ageing process is homogeneous and takes place in an identical manner in every part of the world. According to Szukalski [2014], "this diversity is evident in the scale of individual continents, in accordance with the principle: the higher the standard of living, the greater the chance for longevity and a greater fraction of seniors". The parts of the world where the ageing process occurs most quickly and its negative effects on the socio-economic development can already be seen, are Japan, United States of America and Western Europe.

To measure the progress of the population ageing, demographers, economists and social politicians use numerous indicators. The most popular are traditional measures based on a fixed threshold of old age, established based on the chronological (calendar) age [Abramowska-Kmon 2011]. Using them enables the description of the distribution of population by age, i.e. the age structure of the population and the proportion between the different age groups of the population (see Table 36).

Table 36. Classification of age groups of the population - selected proposals

Category	Age groups
Biological	— 0–14 years — 15–59 years — 60 years and more
Educational	— 3–6 years – pre-school education — 7–12 years – primary education — 13–15 years – lower secondary education — 16–18 years – upper secondary education — 19–24 years – tertiary education
Functional	by five-year groups
Economic	— pre-working age (0–17 years) — working age (18–59/64 years) — mobile age (18–44 years, men and women) — immobile age (45–64 years men and 45–59 years women) — retirement age (60/65 and more)

Source: [*Prognoza ludności* 2008].

Among the indicators used to measure the advancement of ageing of the population also the so-called age factor is often used. It shows the proportion of older individuals (aged 60 or 65 years and over) in the total population[Maj, Jaszczurek 2010]. Far less often used are the so-called alternative measures, taking into account the changing conditions of mortality and referring to the time remaining to death see [Abramowska-Kmon 2011] (Table 37).

Table 37. Stages of ageing due to the median age of the population

The median of age	Rating of the demographic situation
<24 years	Demographically young population
25–29 years	A demographically ageing population
30–34 years	A demographically old population
35 years and more	A demographically very old population

Source: [Okólski 1990].

Among the measures based on the relationships between functional age groups the following factors are also distinguished [Holzer 2003]:

— the overall demographic burden ratio, calculated as the ratio of individuals of non-working age per hundred individuals of working age,

— the senior citizen load ratio, indicating the number of individuals aged 65 years and more per hundred individuals aged 15–64 years,

— the support ratio, i.e. the number of individuals aged 15–64 years per hundred individuals aged 65 years and more,

— the oldest citizen support load ratio, indicating the number of individuals aged 85 years and more per hundred individuals aged 50–64 years.

On the basis of these measures, populations of individual countries or continents are rated as young or old (see Table 38).

Table 38. Selected population age scales

Stages of an population ageing by E. Rosset	
The share of senior citizens (60+)	**Rating of the demographic situation**
Less than 8%	Demographic youth
8–10%	Transition phase
10–12%	Foreground of demographic senility
Over 12%	Demographic senility
Stages of population ageing according to United Nations	
The share of senior citizens (65+)	**Rating of the demographic situation**
Less than 4%	Young population
4–7%	Mature population
Over 7%	Old population

Source: [Rosset, 1959].

The calculations on the UN data conducted by Abramowska-Kmon [2011] and relating to proportion of senior individuals in all countries of the world in the years 1950–2050 show the following distribution of the number of countries according to the Rosset scale:

— currently one third of countries has a population in the phase of demographic senility (one fourth – in the phase of strongly advanced senility), while 19% of countries are in the transition phase,

— in 2050, 80% of the countries will reach the demographic senility phase and 65% will belong to the strongly advanced senility phase.

The analysis of the distribution of the number of countries in the world according to the age scale developed by the United Nations confirms the global nature of the ageing process. In 2010, about 40% of countries had populations in the stage of demographic senility, whereas one-third were at the demographic youth stage. By 2050, the stage of demographic senility will have been reached by 84% of the countries of the world.

The dynamics of the ageing process is assessed on the basis of population growth in the oldest age groups or point changes in their participation. Another way might be the analysis of the time needed to double the share of individuals aged 65 years and over in the population from 7% to 14% [Pison 2009].

However, in the description of the specifics of the ongoing process of ageing it is necessary to exercise caution related to the heterogeneity of the characteristics attributed to a particular chronological (calendar) age. Due to the extension of the period of human life, today sexagenarians are quite different and behave quite differently than their peers at the beginning of the twentieth century. In addition, a sexagenarian living in a country with high level of economic development, providing a high standard of living, cannot be easily compared with individuals of a similar age but living in countries with worse characteristics related to health status, mortality, quality of life and finally, much shorter expected life expectancy (see Figure 22).

According to World Bank data[20], in 2011, the shortest life expectancy was recorded for the inhabitants of the African countries: Swaziland (32 years), Angola (37 years) and Zambia (38 years). In contrast, the longest life expectancy is characteristic for the inhabitants of Andorra (83 years), Japan (82 years) and Singapore (81 years). Already on the basis of these data it appears that the problem of ageing, although global, is uneven and has a different meaning in different countries and regions of the world.

---

[20] http://data.worldbank.org/ (12.01.2014).

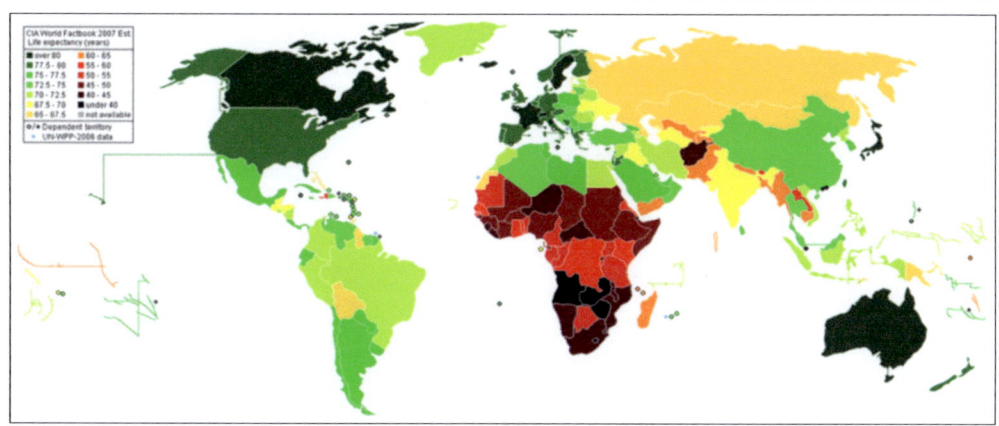

Figure 22. Life expectancy in the world in 2007
Source: http://pl.wikipedia.org/wiki/Plik:Life_Expectancy_2007_Estimates_CIA_World_Fa ctbook.PNG (12.01.2014).

4.2 Expected consequences of the ongoing process of ageing for the economy of some countries of the Baltic Sea Region

The Baltic Sea Region countries (Denmark, Estonia, Finland, Germany, Latvia, Lithuania, Poland and Sweden), as well as all other European countries, are experiencing demographic changes. Two major trends include the ageing of population (defined as a growing number of individuals aged 60 and over in the total population) and declining total population in the perspective of the year 2030. According to forecasts by Eurostat, the process of depopulation touches the Baltic countries, i.e. Latvia, Lithuania and Estonia most. By 2030, the total population of these countries will have decreased compared to the year 2008 by 10%, 8% and 5% respectively. In Poland and Germany, the decrease in the population will not be as significant (respectively 3% and 2.5%). On the other hand, in Denmark, Finland and Sweden the increase of total population is projected (by 6.1%, 5.1% and 11.8% respectively).

Despite the forecasts of total population growth in the Scandinavian countries, also here (outside Sweden) the working age (15–64 years) population will have decreased (see Table 39). The simulations of future demographic changes performed for the Baltic Sea Region at the regional level (NUTS 2) show that only in eight regions there will be a real increase in the share of working-age individuals in the total population and they will include:

— Capital Region of Denmark (DK),

— Stockholm County (SE)

— Hamburg (DE),

— Oberbayern (DE),

— Trier (DE),

— Weser-Ems (DE),

— Sydsverige (SE),

— Västsverige (SE).

Table 39. The change in the population in the 15–64 years age group in the 2008–2030 period in the Baltic Sea Region countries

Country	Change [%]
SE	+2.4
DK	-3.1
FI	-8.2
DE	-12
EE	-13
PL	-14
LT	-15
LV	-17

Source: Eurostat.

Due to the considerable variation of individual countries of the Baltic Sea Region in terms of demographic structure (see Table 40), the level of population activity (see Figure 23), the economic and social situation (including culture and tradition), it is difficult to talk about some common homogeneous socio-economic consequences of ageing in terms of the whole region. What is possible at this point, is merely a classification of these effects. Their intensity and importance will be different in each country.

Table 40. The share of each age group in the population of the Baltic Sea Region (as of 1 January 2012)

Country	0–14 years	15–64 years	65 years and more
		[%]	
DK	17.67	64.97	17.34
DE	13.23	66.13	20.62
EE	15.51	66.78	17.77
LV	14.28	67.15	18.56
LT	14.78	67.12	18.08
PL	15.09	71.08	13.81
FI	16.45	65.40	18.13
SE	16.70	64.47	18.81

Source: Eurostat.

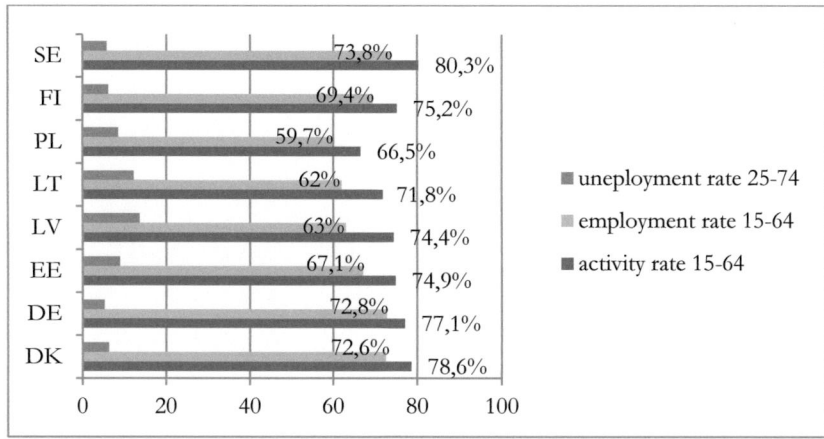

Figure 23. Selected indicators of economic activity in the countries of the Baltic Sea Region (as of 1 January 2012)
Source: own work on the basis of Eurostat data.

Among the risks associated with the ageing of the population, the danger of public finance instability is mentioned most frequently. It involves, among others:

— growing costs of pension benefits and the growing number of retirees,
— increased spending on health and social care of senior citizens,
— reduced budget revenues from income taxes, as a result of the decreasing number of the economically active individuals.

When Bismarck created his social security system, the retirement age was reached by few workers, and if they did reach it, they died rather soon. Now, in light of the observed change of demographic regime, reaching the retirement age is almost "certain" and the period of professional inactivity in retirement is longer and longer.

In 2011, nearly 60% of the retired respondents from Poland had not reached the statutory retirement age by the time of their retirement yet[21]. Among men, the figure was 65.0%, whereas among women — 52.0%. In turn, persons who died in 2011 had been receiving their pensions for 16 years and 2 months on average. Men received their pension for 15 years and 4 months on average, whereas women for over two years longer. A slightly shorter period of receiving pension by women was observed only in the 56–60 age group. The dominant interval period of retirement payout

---

[21] At the time of the study, the statutory retirement age in Poland was 60 years for women and 65 for men.

among both men and women was 16–20 years [*Analiza wyników badania* 2012](see Figure 24).

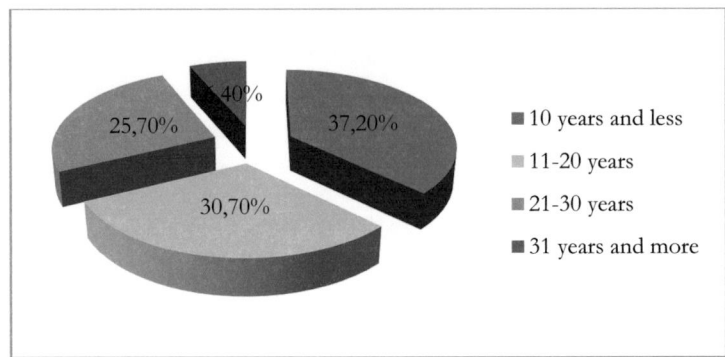

Figure 24. The structure of pensions according to the length of their payout period
Source: [*Analiza wyników badania* 2012].

According to the report of the European Commission [The 2012 Aging Report 2012], in the 2010–2060 period, the public expenditure of 27 Member States of the European Union in respect of pension payments will increase by 1.5 percentage points, i.e. to 12% of GDP (Gross Domestic Product). In the BSR countries, the growth of this category of spending is projected for Germany, Lithuania, Finland and Sweden (see Table 41).

Table 41. Change in gross public pension expenditure over 2010-2060 (in p.p. of GDP)

Country	2010	2020	2040	2060	Change 2010–2060
DK	10.1	10.8	10.3	9.5	-0.6
DE	10.8	10.9	12.7	13.4	2.6
EE	8.9	7.7	8.1	7.7	-1.1
LV	9.7	7.3	6.3	5.9	-3.8
LT	8.6	7.6	9.6	12.1	3.5
PL	11.8	10.9	10.3	9.6	-2.2
FI	12.0	14.0	15.2	15.2	5.2
SE	9.6	9.6	10.2	10.2	0.6

Source: [*The 2012 Ageing Report* 2012].

Another source of growing public expenditures is the costs associated with health and social care. In 2009, the total health expenditure in the 27 Member States of the European Union amounted to 10.2% of GDP. The public expenditure for this purpose constituted 7.8% of GDP. The BSR countries show a great diversity in terms of health care spending. The largest expenditure (calculated as a percentage of GDP or percentage of total public expenditure) is born by the Scandinavian countries and Germany. New EU Member States (Estonia, Latvia, Lithuania and Poland) commit significantly lower funds to this type of public services.

Table 42. Public health care expenditure (including long-term nursing care) in Baltic Sea Region Countries in 2009

Country	Public health care expenditure as % of		
	GDP	Total health expenditure	Total government expenditure
DK	9.8	85	15
DE	8.9	77	14.4
EE	5.3	75	12.4
LV	4.1	62	10.6
LT	5.6	73	12.8
PL	5.3	72	11.5
FI	6.8	75	14.2
SE	8.2	81	13.4

Source: own calculation on the basis of Eurostat data.

The amount of expenditure in this category is determined by a number of factors. The demand side includes the size of the population, its age structure, the quality of health care (including prevention), affluence and access to health services. In turn, the supply side is determined by the formal and legal solutions for the organization and financing of the health care system or the level of technological development.

The ageing population is also a threat to labour markets. The decreasing number of individuals in the so-called *prime age* constitutes a risk of limited access to qualified personnel — in turn, the increasing the number of individuals approaching retirement age results in the need for the customization of workplaces/jobs (e.g. within the dimension of more flexible organization of work or ensuring appropriate ergonomic conditions in the workplace) to the needs of seniors.

The provision of human capital in the quantities required by the labour market in the coming decades will necessitate taking a number of actions aimed at activating the groups traditionally remaining on its margins. Active labour market integration of i.a. more women, the disabled, seniors (including those who exceeded the formal retirement age), immigrants etc. is meant here. The actions aimed at securing the right amount of human capital will have to be accompanied by measures aimed at ensuring the appropriate level of their quality. This means i.a. the need for investment in education, training systems and various forms of counselling.

Box 1. Public health care expenditure in the last decades

The governments of all EU Member States are heavily involved in the financing and often in the provision of health care services. Public health care spending is a major and growing source of fiscal pressure, representing a significant and growing share of GDP in EU Member States.

During the 1960s and 1970s, public (and private) health care expenditure rose rapidly, triggered by an increase in population coverage and improvements in the provision of the health services associated with populations' higher expectations and their willingness to pay more for better health care services. In the 1980s and 1990s, the growth of public expenditure on health slowed down, and even reversed in a few countries. This was largely due to budgetary consolidation efforts, as growth in health care expenditure was perceived as too strong. In the late 1990s and especially in the first decade of the 21st century, health expenditure growth picked up again. It has reached an average level of 8% of GDP in 2009 in the EU, though ranging from less than 3% of GDP in Cyprus to nearly 10% of GDP in Denmark.

As far as the share of public in total health expenditure is concerned, there seem to be two divergent movements: in general, the share of public spending in EU15 Member States has increased in the last decade, whilst in EU12 Member States private financing has increased as a source of total health care funding. Moreover, health care has gained prominence relative to other government expenditure. In all EU Member States with available data except for Hungary, Romania, Austria and Portugal, the share of health care in total government expenditure has increased. Public spending on health care now accounts on average for 14.6% of total government spending in the EU, ranging from 7.2 to 18.8%. 75% of the EU Member States spend between 11 to 15% of their resources on health care.

Source: [*The 2012 Ageing Report* 2012].

In the perspective of the year 2030, the European Commission predicts two phases of changes in the labour market [*The 2012 Aging Report* 2012]:

— in the period 2013 – 2021 – *rising employment rate offsets the decline in the working-age population*: the working-age population starts to decline as the baby-boom generation enters retirement. However, the assumed reduction in unemployment rates, the projected increase in the employment rates of women and older workers cushion the impact of demographic change, and the overall number of persons employed would continue to increase, albeit at a slower pace;

— from the year 2022 – *the ageing effect dominates* – the trend increase in female employment rates will broadly have worked itself through. In absence of further reforms, the employment rate of older workers is also projected to reach a steady state. Consequently, there is no counter-balancing factor to ageing, and both the working-age population and the number of persons employed enter a downward trajectory.

In order to assess the impact of demographic change on the state of the economies of countries and regions in Europe, as well as the risks of further development, the Rostocker Zentrum zur Erforschung des Demografischen Wandels developed the Regional Demographic Change Index (RDC) and the Regional Demographic Location Risk measure (RDLR).

RDC allows a comparison of demographic change across regions or countries and between periods [Tivig et al. 2008]. It is built on the basis of information about ageing and shrinking, the two dimensions of demographic change. Ageing is thereby measured as increase in mean age and shrinking as a negative growth rate of population. The RDC Index takes values between 0 (weakest RDC) and 1 (strongest RDC). Intermediate values are interpreted as "weakest demographic change (DC)", if they are lower than 0.2; as "weak DC" if they range between 0.2 and 0.4; as "moderate DC" it they lie in the interval 0.4–0.6; as "strong DC" if they fall into the range 0.6–0.8; and finally as "strongest DC" if they lie above 0.8.

Calculations for the 76 NUTS 2 Baltic Sea regions considered over the period of 2008–2030 with data from the 2008 Eurostat population projection yielded an Index value of 0.0 for Hamburg, Trier (both Germany), Stockholm and Sydsverige (both Sweden). An RDC Index value close to 1.0 is assigned to four German regions: Sachsen-Anhalt: 0.94; Brandenburg–Nordost: 0.96; Thüringen: 0.97, and Dresden: 1.0 [Tivig, Korb 2012]. The condensed characteristics of the Baltic Sea Region countries on the basis of the RDC are presented in Table 43.

Table 43. Characteristics of the Baltic Sea Region countries based on RDC

DK	Demographic change in Denmark's regions is expected to be weak all over except for the capital, which is likely to experience weakest demographic change in the period of 2008–2030. RDC Index values range from 0.15 for Hovedstaden to 0.37 for Nordjylland
DE	The spread of future regional RDC Index values is projected to be high. It ranges from 0.0 to 1.0 and hence from lowest to highest values. Eleven out of the 39 German NUTS 2 regions are expected to display strongest demographic change, meaning RDC Index values of 0.8 and higher, while only five German regions are projected to experience weakest demographic change, implying a RDC Index value of less than 0.2.
EE, LV, LT	Demographic change in Latvia and Lithuania will be strong between 2008 and 2030, while it is expected moderate in Estonia. The RDC Index takes the values: 0.49 for Estonia, 0.67 for Latvia and 0.72 for Lithuania. Ageing and shrinking contribute both to these results.
FI	The intensity of demographic change in the five Finnish regions is expected weakest for

	Lland with a RDC Index value of 0.14 and strongest for Itä-Suomi with 0.66. Etelä-Suomi, Länsi-Suomi and Pohjois-Suomi will experience weak demographic change as well; the RDC Index values are estimated to lie between 0.22 and 0.31.
PL	In Poland, there are only two out of the 16 regions which are likely to show moderate demographic change: the capital region Mazowieckie with a RDC Index value of 0.51, and Pomorskie with 0.59. All other regions are expected to experience strong to strongest DC, the RDC Index values ranging from 0.66 for Małopolskie to 0.93 for Swietokrzyskie.
SE	Swedish regions show weak to weakest demographic change. The Northern regions are expected to see weak demographic change with RDC Index values lying between 0.27 and 0.33; values for the other five regions lie below 0.16

Source: [Tivig, Korb 2012].

Regional Demographic Location Risk (RDLR) is less straightforward than RDC. It considers demographic, location and contextual factors. A so-called "demographic component" (*Dem*) is thereby linked to a "location component" (*Loc*) to result in a composite indicator *DemLoc*. The former accounts for the pattern, extent and timing of demographic change, the latter depicts the current state of a location factor in a region. Indicators for three contextual factors (*Con*) are then added, reflecting other regional characteristics that are believed to influence the *DemLoc* link. The selection of factors and valuation of their interaction in generating Regional Demographic Location Risk have been based on expert assessment [Tivig et al. 2008]. RDLR measure allows assessing risks and opportunities resulting from the concurrence of demographic trends, location characteristics and contextual influences in a region. It is provided as an aggregate measure as well as separately for labour supply, human capital, productivity and R&D. Values range from -5 to +5. Negative values indicate risks, positive values opportunities, intermediate positions are scored 0.

The most adverse levels of the Regional Demographic Location Risk index among the Baltic Sea Region countries are present in the new Member States. This is particularly evident in the "labour and productivity" and "R & D" areas (see Table 44).

Table 44. Average values of the RDLR index for the Baltic Sea Region countries

Country	Labour supply	Human capital	Labour productivity	R&D
DK	- 2	+ 5	+ 3	+ 4
DE	- 0.6	- 1.8	- 0.3	+ 2.8
EE	- 4	+ 2	- 5	- 3
LV	- 5	- 1	- 4	- 5
LT	- 4	+ 4	- 5	- 5
PL	- 0.9	- 2.5	- 4	- 5
FI	- 1	+ 4	+ 0.4	+ 2.7
SE	+ 1.6	+ 2.1	+ 0.6	+ 1.5

Source: own calculations based on [Tivig et al. 2008].

Demographic changes bring also other economic and social consequences. One of them is the development of *silver economy*, i.e. an economic system aimed at exploiting the potential of seniors and meeting their needs, already noticeable in the Western Europe.

Despite the complexity of the concept, the most common analysis of the *silver economy* narrows down to the consumer market, where individuals aged 60+ are the target group of customers, and the enterprise offers (including the methods of reaching and serving the customer) are designed and tailored to their needs. The development of the *silver economy* is also related to the growing number of seniors — potential clients — and the relatively high purchasing power they represent. According to statistics presented during the *Kilkenny Business of Ageing Forum* in September 2010 and listed in *The business of ageing – turning silver into gold* portal:[22]

— 80% of the UK's wealth is held by people aged over 50 years old,
— wealth and revenues in Europe of persons over 65 is over 3 trillion EURO,
— the over fifties in Europe have around 70% of all savings and represent the market for inheritance products and services,
— two thirds of homeowners over 60 in the UK getting by on under 10000 pounds a year and they have over 841 billion pounds or an average of 82446 pounds each, tied up in bricks and mortar.

In the United States, the elderly — especially from the *older baby boomers* group — spend [*Demographic Profile* 2006]:

— more than 10% above the average for the purchases of image-shaping goods and services (clothes, cosmetics, beauty salon services, aesthetic medicine, etc.),
— 23% above the average for hotels and holiday trips,
— 20% above the average for health and personal insurance.

For most of today's sexagenarians, being sixty means as much as being forty a few decades ago. The older people remain more active physically and socially. In the United States, the daily use of the Internet is declared by 72% of people aged 51–59 years and 54% of those aged 60–69 years. In addition, the American *baby boomers* [*Business Innovation Factory* 2010]:

— make purchases online – 68%,
— check e-mail every day – 42%,
— enjoy online games – 25%,

---

[22] http://www.businessofageing.com/www/default/index.cfm (10/10/2010).

— read blogs – 21%.

D. Stround [2005] in his book *The 50-plus market* talks about the so-called *charmed generation*. It is the people of Western Europe, retired or soon to retire, achieving very high income. According to Stround, never in the future will there appear so large and so financially affluent a group of retirees.

The ageing population also means a change in other areas, including the education system. The decreasing number of individuals under 20 forces educational institutions — including universities — to develop their educational offer. This is done in two ways:

— by adapting education to the needs of an ageing population (e.g. in such specialties as senior citizen caregiver, andragogy etc.)
— by adapting the educational offer to the needs of the seniors themselves (e.g. retraining courses, universities of the third age etc.).

To conclude the reasoning contained in the chapter, it can be stated unequivocally that in the context of the ongoing process of population ageing in Europe, the economic situation in the Baltic Sea Region will be changing. The changes will be related to the labour market, the consumer goods market and the market of public services, as well as to the education systems. The growing proportion of older people in the total population means on the one hand the need to develop innovative solutions (providing the desired high productivity offsetting the lower availability of human capital) within the area of production — the supply of goods and services — and on the other, ensuring a system that would provide a high quality of life for seniors.

The problems related to the expected changes necessary to take actions have been covered in the main strategic documents of the European Union relating directly to the Baltic Sea Region. Among other things, the Strategy for the Baltic Sea Region states that "the achievement of high productivity, high levels of innovation and sustainable economic growth in the Baltic Sea Region requires an increase in the scope of social inclusion and integration in the labour market". In turn, the competitiveness and attractiveness of the region depends on such important factors as high levels of employment, good jobs, the continued presence of a skilled and flexible workforce, as well as low levels of social exclusion [*European Union Strategy for the Baltic Sea Region* 2009]. The efforts aimed at solving the socio-economic problems expected as a consequence of demographic changes engage almost all organizational structures centred around the Baltic Sea Region, including: Council of the Baltic Sea States[23], Baltic Sea

---

[23] Council of the Baltic Sea States (CBSS) was established by the conference of the BSR Foreign Ministers (with the participation of the EU) in 1992 (plus Iceland who joined in 1995) as a response to the

States Sub regional Cooperation[24], Baltic Sea Parliamentary Conference[25], Baltic Sea Forum[26], Baltic Development Forum[27] and The Baltic Sea Labour Forum (BSLF)[28].

4.3. The problems of enterprises in the face of an ageing population

The ageing of population produces specific changes in the macroeconomic dimension and in the society as a collectivity. Equal attention should be paid, however, to the analysis of their importance in the micro-economic dimension, i.e. for individual companies.

geopolitical changes occurring in the BSR with the end of the Cold War. The CBSS focuses on the need for increasing cooperation among the BSR countries and attempts, first of all, to secure democracy and to achieve balanced economic development. Its main aim is to identify political goals, create action plans, initiate projects and provide a forum for the exchange of ideas in respect of regional issues of common interest; http://www.cbss.org

[24] Baltic Sea States Subregional Cooperation (BSSSC) is a political network for decentralized authorities (sub-regions) in the BSR, founded in 1993 with strong cooperative links with other BSR and European organizations. Its mission is oriented to permanently strengthening the BSR image in order for it to become an important player in the broader European scenario. As a Pan-Baltic organization it is open to all BSR regions without distinction. By making use of its political status and by being a close partner to the CBSS, it intends to promote regions, decision makers, national governments, EU and even global interests; http://www.bsssc.com

[25] Baltic Sea Parliamentary Conference (BSPC) is the parliamentary forum of the BSR. Its main aim is to increase cooperation between the parliamentary institutions of the BSR both on a regional and a national level in order to facilitate the bases for the discussion of major regional issues. In their annual sessions, the presidency of the CBSS actively participates by presenting the work programme of that organization; http://www.bspc.net

[26] Baltic Sea Forum is a private non governmental organisation which works together with a number of governments as well as with state-wide, regional and local institutions. It possesses a representative network of members from the business world, politics and administration and is oriented to promoting economic and cultural cooperation; to support the EU's Northern Dimension Action Plan and EU projects; to provide an independent scenario for the exchange of ideas; to improve information flows within the region; and to consult political institutions on how to reduce obstacles to regional cooperation. Led by an international executive board, it maintains offices in all BSR countries, plus Brussels and Switzerland

[27] Baltic Development Forum is an independent non-profit networking organization oriented towards the development of new initiatives, public-private partnerships and international contacts as a way to stimulate growth, innovation and competitiveness in the BSR. Its mission is to develop the BSR as a global centre of excellence and to establish the region internationally as a strong and attractive place brand with a dynamic business environment. Members include a wide range of partners including large companies, major cities, institutional investors, regional organizations, research and media institutions and business associations across the BSR; http://www.bdforum.org

[28] The Baltic Sea Labour Forum is a platform for exchange of experience and communication between the key labour market actors in the Baltic Sea Region. It brings together the key labour market actors from around the Baltic Sea Region; http://www.bslf.eu/

According to Frosch, Kühntopf and Tivig (2008), demographic change matters for firms to the extent that it influences their activities. An ageing and shrinking population involves changes in the demand for consumption goods, housing and services. On the supply side, labour is the ultimate resource. If ageing and shrinking of total population translates into ageing and shrinking of the labour force, firms resent it. A study involving 99 European regions showed that shrinking of the labour force is much more pronounced than shrinking of total population, whereas for ageing it is the other way round. Hence, while population ageing is the main issue for individuals and societies until 2030, for firms it is shrinking of the labour force. But ageing and shrinking interact, so that the former will increasingly impact firms, too.

This means that in the enterprise perspective, implications of an ageing population can be analysed in at least two ways:
— the inputs and outputs of the enterprise as an socio-economic system (see Figure 25),
— the internal organization of the enterprise.

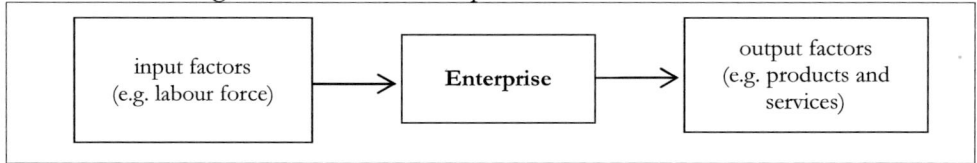

Figure 25. Enterprise inputs and outputs
Source: own work.

Due to the ongoing demographic changes in the environment, enterprises will change the characteristics of selected streams of inputs and outputs. In the perspective of shrinking labour force, mainly the access to skilled workers in the so-called *prime age* will be reduced. The labour resources available in the market will be represented mainly by individuals approaching retirement age (input side). The modifications on the output side will, in turn, be a consequence of the growing number of older consumers — they will focus on adapting the offer (products and services) to the needs of this group of buyers [Wassel 2011, p. 351-360]. The changes will also cover such areas of business activity as the system of communication with customers, pricing strategies, organization of supply or after-sales service.

In terms of the internal organization of an enterprise, the ageing of population will necessitate the implementation of new management methods. Among others, solutions adjusting the conditions and organization of work to the needs of older people and ensuring high productivity of enterprises, offsetting the quantitative and qualitative deficits in the labour force, are meant here.

Therefore, enterprises are increasingly turning to the implementation of the concept of age management. It is most commonly associated with the management of ageing workers and increasing the flexibility of the working conditions of that group in order to preserve (prolong) its economic activity [Litwiński, Sztanderska 2010]. In broader terms, this means optimizing the utilization of the potential of the diversity of employees, mainly in terms of age but also gender, educational profile etc. Age management understood in this way involves [Jaworski, 2010], [Schimanek 2010]:

— comprehensive, holistic approach to employee development and career path,
— career and development management, including the system of education and training, motivating,
— organizing work in a manner appropriate to the specifics of employees of this age, their health and family commitments, also through proper organization of the workplace, flexible working hours and types of employment,
— taking into account the phases of human life cycle by adjusting the professional (employee) roles adequately.

Age management is not limited to creating optimal working conditions for older workers. It means managing employees of all ages, while paying special attention to old age. The age management methodology, besides the already discussed aspects, enables also the provision of an intergenerational transfer of knowledge and skills specific to given organizations. In this way, the risk of a competence gap and loss of the distinctive competences of the enterprise can be avoided [Ilmarinen 2005].

The ageing of the labour force in the enterprise perspective will be also connected with the necessity of investing. There will be projects both involving adapting workplaces/jobs to the needs of older workers (the growing importance of ergonomics in the organization of work) and ensuring appropriate business productivity. As Wojciechowski [2014] writes, an increase in labour productivity can be achieved by increasing the rate of investment in the economy. Higher capital expenditures contribute to faster economic growth not only directly but also indirectly, because the increase in investment promotes the adaptation of innovations that increase the productivity of capital.

> **Box 2. Age management's dimensions**
>
> Age management is not purely and simply about preventing age discrimination, changing attitudes and promoting age diversity. Certainly, it encompasses these actions. But age management implies reaching beyond the conventional policy instruments of the human resources department for practical means whereby the older worker may have a greater and more sustained impact and value to the organization.
>
> The following eight dimensions have been identified as falling within the age management sphere of interest:
> — Job recruitment
> — Learning, training and lifelong learning
> — Career development
> — Flexible working time practices
> — Health protection and promotion and workplace design
> — Redeployment
> — Employment exit and transition to retirement
> — Comprehensive approaches.
>
> To the above, the following additional categories may be added as having sometimes been used by the same writers — though to a degree they may overlap with the foregoing:
> — Changing attitudes
> — Ergonomics and job design
> — Wage policy.
>
> Source: [Naegele, Walker 2006]

According to the studies carried out by different centres [Czernecka, Woszczyk 2013; Lichtarski, Wąsowicz, Stańczyk-Hugiet 2014; Liwiński 2010; Liwiński, Sztanderska 2013; *Szanse i bariery* 2009], the Polish enterprises still remain unprepared to demographic changes. Many entrepreneurs are not aware of the future situation in the labour market. In times of crisis, entrepreneurs and managers are more focused on reducing costs (including laying off employees) and limiting investment than on developig new methods of managing employees, the more so the ones focused on the future status of employment [Richert-Kaźmierska 2013]. This does not change the fact that the implementation of new solutions sooner or later will become a necessity. The offsetting of deficits in the field of age management instruments may be served well by the transfer of good practices from the countries in which enterprises have been implementing this concept for years. In the sixth chapter of this book some of such practices are presented. It seems that the proven examples should help Polish enterprises, lacking experience in age management, in finding their own way to solve the problems they will have to face in the coming decades.

References

1. Abramowska-Kmon A. (2011) *O nowych miarach zaawansowania procesu starzenia się ludności*, „Studia demograficzne" Nr 1(159).
2. *Analiza wyników badania okresów pobierania emerytur* (2012), Zakład Ubezpieczeń Społecznych Departament Statystyki i Prognoz Aktuarialnych, Warszawa.
3. *Business Innovation Factory. Nursing Home of the Future*, http://www.businessinnovationfactory.com /nhf/files/Boomers.pdf (10/10/2010).
4. Czernecka M., Woszczyk P. (2013) *Człowiek to inwestycja, Podręcznik do zarządzania wiekiem w organizacjach*, HRP Group, Łódź.
5. *Demographic Profile. American Baby Boomers* (2006), Mature Market Institute, Metropolitan Life Insurance Company, New York.
6. *European Union Strategy for the Baltic Sea Region* (2009), Communication from the Commission to the European Parliament, the Council, the European Economic and Social Committee and the Committee of the Regions, Brussels, 10.6.2009 COM (2009) 248, final version.
7. Holzer J.Z. (2003) *Demografia*, Polskie Wydawnictwo Ekonomiczne, Warszawa.
8. http://www.businessofageing.com/www/default/index.cfm (10/10/2010).
9. http://data.worldbank.org/ (12.01.2014).
10. Ilmarinen J. (2005) *Towards a longer worklife! Ageing and the quality of worklife in the European Union*, Finnish Institute of Occupational Health, Ministry of Social Affairs and Health, Helsinki.
11. Jaworska J. (2010) *Rola pracodawców w strategiach wydłużania aktywności zawodowej osób 50+*, in: *Zarządzanie wiekiem i nie tylko*, Akademia Rozwoju Filantropii w Polsce, Warszawa.
12. Lichtarski J., Wąsowicz M., Stańczyk-Hugiet E., *Raport na temat możliwości wykorzystania nowoczesnych metod zarządzania, w tym zarządzania wiedzą w obszarze aktywizacji osób starszych*, http://www.silverteam.dobrekadry.pl/dokumenty/Raport nt mozliwosci wyko rzystania metod zarzadzania %282%29.pdf (12.02.2014).
13. Liwiński J. (2010) *Opis dobrych praktyk dotyczących zarządzania wiekiem w przedsiębiorstwach polskich oraz innych krajów UE*, PARP, .
14. Litwiński J., Sztanderska U. (2010) *Wstępne standardy zarządzania wiekiem w przedsiębiorstwach*, PARP, Warszawa.
15. Liwiński J., Sztanderska U. (2013) *Standardy zarządzania wiekiem w organizacjach*, PARP, Warszawa.
16. Maj K., Jaszczurek S. (2010) *Słownik Geografia*, Greg.
17. Okólski M. (ed.) (1990) *Teoria przejścia demograficznego*, PWE, Warszawa.

18. Pison G. (2009) *Le vieillissement demographique sera plus rapide au Sud qu'au Nord*, „Population and Societes" no. 457.
19. *Prognoza ludności na lata 2008-2035*, GUS, Warszawa 2008, http://demografia.stat.gov.pl/bazademografia/Prognoza.aspx (12.01.2014).
20. Racław M., Rosochacka-Gmitrzak M. (2012) *Proces starzenia się, w kontekście wyzwań demografii, polityki społecznej oraz doniesień badawczych*, Ekspertyza wykonana na zlecenie Ministerstwa Pracy i Polityki Społecznej, Warszawa, http://www.wrzos.org.pl/download/Ekspertyza_1_ASOS.pdf (12.01.2014).
21. Richert-Kaźmierska A. (2013) *Is There any Demand for the Workers Aged 50+ in Poland?* Equilibrium Volume 8, Issue 3.
22. Rosset E. (1959) *Proces starzenia się ludności. Studium demograficzne*, Polskie Wydawnictwa Gospodarcze, Warszawa.
23. Stround D. (2005) *The 50-plus market*, Kogan Page Limited, London.
24. Schimanek T. (2010) *Co to jest zarządzanie wiekiem?*, (in:) *Zarządzanie wiekiem i nie tylko*, Akademia Rozwoju Filantropii w Polsce, Warszawa.
25. *Szanse i bariery zatrudniania osób w wieku 45+ w województwie pomorskim. Raport końcowy* (2009) Wojewódzki Urząd Pracy w Gdańsku, Gdańsk.
26. Szukalski P., *Zagrożenie czy wyzwanie – proces starzenia się ludności*, Materiał roboczy w repozytorium Uniwersytetu Łódzkiego, http://dspace.uni.lodz.pl:8080/xmlui/bitstream/handle/11089/3456/PS%202006-9.pdf?sequence=1 (12.01.2014).
27. *The 2012 Ageing Report Economic and budgetary projections for the 27 EU Member States (2010-2060)*(2012), Joint Report prepared by the European Commission (DG ECFIN) and the Economic Policy Committee (AWG), European Economy 2.
28. Tivig T., Frosch K., Kühntopf S. (2008) *Mapping Regional Demographic Change and Regional Demographic Location Risk in Europe*, Rostock Center for the Study of Demographic Change Rostock, 2008.
29. Tivig T., Korb C. (2012) *Work Participation and Employability of Best Agers in the Baltic Sea Region. Final Report*, Rostock.
30. Wassel J.I. (2011) *Business and ageing: the boomer effect on consumers and marketing* (in:) Settersten R.A., Angel J.L. (ed.), *Handbook of sociology of aging*, Springer, New York.
31. Wojciechowski W., *Wyzwania dla rynku pracy wynikające ze starzenia się społeczeństw*, http://liberte.pl/wyzwania-dla-rynku-pracy-wynikajace-ze-starzenia-sie-spoleczenstw/ (20.02.2014).
32. *The 2012 Ageing Report Economic and budgetary projections for the 27 EU Member States (2010-2060)*. Joint Report prepared by the European Commission (DG ECFIN) and the Economic Policy Committee (AWG), European Economy 2/2012.
33. T. Tivig, C. Korb, *Work Participation and Employability of Best Agers in the Baltic Sea Region. Final Report*, Rostock 2012.

34. T. Tivig, K. Frosch, S. Kühntopf, *Mapping Regional Demographic Change and Regional Demographic Location Risk in Europe*, Rostock Center for the Study of Demographic Change Rostock, 2008.
35. G. Naegele, A. Walker (2006), A Guide to Good Practice in Age Management, European Foundation, Dublin, www.eurofound.europa.eu/areas/populationand society/ageingworkforce.htm (12.01.2014).

Chapter V Social inclusion policy in the perspective of building the competitiveness of enterprises

5. 1. Disadvantaged groups in the labour market

The concept of social exclusion has lived to see many definitions, hence the desire for synthetic perspective of threads discussed by different authors. Such attempts were made in the European Union Poverty3 [Andersen at all in 1994, p. 10–11] evaluation report. It has been assumed in it that social exclusion is a dynamic, multidimensional process consisting of different stages and phases, as well as:

1. is often caused by a lack of resources;
2. it often leads to multidimensional deprivation of various degrees of intensity;
3. it has aspects both reflected by monetary indicators, as well as ones not captured by indicators;
4. it is characterized by deficits of participation (of varying intensity) in mainstream society and access to essential social systems (labour market, social security, education, health care);
5. it produces potential threat of breaking ties with the family and the society or causing loss of sense of identity and purpose in life;
6. it is associated with deprivation of or not availing of social rights;
7. it includes consolidating factors, which carries the risk of duplication of behaviour model, also between generations (the so-called "inheritance").

Social exclusion is not a new phenomenon — it is determined by identifying deficits of participation in important aspects of collective life (social, economic, political, cultural or other, characteristic for a given society). The reasons for lack of participation can be very diverse — it may be the cause or consequence of social exclusion.

Researchers dealing with issues of social exclusion focus their attention on certain social categories at risk of exclusion. Silver [Silver 1995, p. 74–75] presented a list of 23 such categories, which include both women and the elderly. It should also be noted that these categories are not disjoint and exclusion is often associated with the accumulation of several factors. Much attention is paid to specific social groups or individuals confronted with specific problems. These excluded groups include, for example: young people, women, people over 50 years of age, the long-term unemployed, people in rural areas, the disabled, mentally ill, immigrants and minority groups, homeless or inmates leaving prisons.

Some researchers suggest that social exclusion may be related to limitation of social rights. It turns out, however, that even the universality of social rights does not guarantee access to key institutions of collective life, which was proved by Atkinson [Atkinson, Hills 1998], who highlighted the relationships between poverty, unemployment and social exclusion.

Typically, people disadvantaged in the labour market underline the significant role that work plays in their lives: first of all in satisfying their financial needs, but also in providing human contact and contributing to the achievement of satisfaction with the good performance of tasks or self-actualization. Research conducted by Pentor [Rusin, Sobolewska Bujko 2010, p. 12–14] has shown that more than ¾ of the respondents did not work professionally, with the highest percentage observed among the long-term unemployed, and the lowest – among single mothers. The working respondents were usually employed temporarily. It is a hallmark of disadvantaged groups in the labour market, which further increases their feeling of uncertainty and fear of losing their jobs. Typically, loss of employment causes falling into the state of long-term unemployment (over 2 years). In addition to the loss of livelihood, lack of work also causes the deterioration of the mental health of the disadvantaged. A major problem is passivity – about 20% of unemployed respondents did not take any action to take up employment. Using family and social contacts was indicated as the most effective job search method. A number of barriers to seeking and getting a job were also identified (see Table 45).

Table 45. Barriers in the labour market

Types of barriers in the labour market	Main barriers	Consequences
Personal	Educational (low level of education, lack of skills and difficulties with raising them, lack of knowledge of new technologies, lack of knowledge of job search methods) Psychological (low self-esteem, lack of self-confidence) Economical (difficult financial situation, lack of means for an active job search) Health problems (chronic illness, addictions)	Learned helplessness (waiving further action) External locus of control (a feeling that one has no influence on one's own fate) The self-fulfilling prophecy (conduct consistent with stereotypes)
External	Stereotyping (fear of employing people perceived from the angle of the negative elements of the stereotype) Systemic limitations (system of determining disability and/or inability to work, the pension system, lack of nurseries and kindergartens in the context of actual needs, making it difficult to take up employment for single mothers) Jobs for the disadvantaged (small number of offers, unfavourable financial and working conditions)	

5. 2. Assumptions of the European policy of economic and social inclusion

Despite many efforts made by governments, states and international organizations, the problem of poverty and social exclusion remains a malady of many countries. Research in this area indicates the complexity and multidimensionality of issues, which necessitates taking measures aimed at reducing the scale of the phenomenon by different actors at different levels. They often require an integrated approach, too.

Deep regional diversity is not only an obstacle to achieving economic and social cohesion in Europe, but also frequently undermines the development efforts of individual countries.

Social exclusion, closely related to the concept of poverty, has become an important social and political category of the European Union. It has been recognized as a significant barrier to economic growth and sustainable development, but also drew attention to the threat that it poses to society.

As part of the social activities in the European Union, and earlier in the European Community, a number of programmes were implemented.

The first of these was established by resolution of the Council of the European Communities in 1974 — its main aim was described as: "full and better employment at Community, national and regional levels, which is an essential condition for an effective social policy; improvement of living and working conditions so as to make possible their harmonization while the improvement is being maintained; increased involvement of management and labour in the economic and social decisions of the Community, and of workers in the life of undertakings... ". This programme was originally valid until 1976 — then it was extended until 1979 and supplemented by an additional program lasting until 1981. The resolution also expressed the political will to implement and set priorities for [Council of the European Communities 1974, p. 8–10]:

— attainment of full and better employment in the Community;
— improvement of living and working conditions so as to make possible their harmonization while the increased involvement of management and labour in the economic and social decisions of the Community, and of workers in the life of undertakings improvement is being maintained.

It was found, however, that greater wealth does not mean solving social problems and sometimes can even exacerbate them. Some regions or groups will not be participating in the general progress fully and as a result will be falling further behind [Council of the European Communities 1974, p. 13].

Another programme was implemented in the years 1985–1988 with a budget of 25 million ECU [Council Decision 1985]. The beneficiaries were people with disabilities, the long-term unemployed, the young unemployed, the elderly immigrants, refugees and repatriates, the homeless and the seniors in general. Funding has also received by Eurostat for the development of poverty indicators.

The third programme covered the years 1989–1994 and involved the continuation and extension of the of the previous programme activities. The term *poverty* was replaced in it by the term *economic and social exclusion*. It also identified the need to ensure economic and social cohesion by: „taking preventive measures against any short-term negative effects of completion of the large market on the social groups most at risk and optimizing corrective measures for the groups already marginalized" [Council Decision 1989, p. 0010].

Great importance was also attributed to the horizontal coordination and innovation activities of non-governmental organizations working on the inclusion of groups subject to various forms of isolation.

On the other hand, the European Commission proposal from 1993 concerning arranging medium term actions aimed at counteracting exclusion, promoting social solidarity, as well as supporting and promoting innovations, was rejected. As a result, the money allocated for this purpose has been allocated among the European Social Fund and pro-employment projects [Szarfenberg 2009, p. 4].

In a resolution adopted in 1989 by the European Council and the Ministers of Social Affairs it was stressed that "combating the social exclusion may be regarded as an important part of the social dimension of the international market". Limited access to the labour market was indicated as the main cause of exclusion. [Council Resolution 1989] The Member States were requested to take steps towards enabling all interested individuals access to education, training, employment, utilities, medical care and housing.

For this reason, it is worth paying attention to the two recommendations of the European Community from 1992:

1) on common criteria for sufficient resources and social assistance in social protection systems (social protection, now translated as social security) [Council Recommendation 1992, 441]

2) on the convergence of objectives and policies of social protection [Council Recommendation 1992, 442].

The European Commission presented only one report on the implementation of the first of the recommendations in the Member States. The main conclusions are presented below [European Community 1998, p. 5–13].

1. The minimum income (the subsistence wage) secured only basic needs during financial crisis.
2. The minimum income programs were usually parts of the social benefits system.
3. In 12 Member States readiness to take up work or training was required from their beneficiaries. The ill, the disabled, as well as carers of the sick or disabled, were exempted from this obligation.
4. In half of the Member States measures of social integration were combined with employment training (the participants were allowed to combine receiving the benefit with gainful employment).
5. Expenditure on the benefits related to the provision of minimum income is small compared with the total expenditure for social purposes, and for a large group of beneficiaries they are the only source of income.
6. An increase in the number of job seekers and people who have found themselves in a difficult situation has been observed. Most of them were men or incomplete families who collected the minimum income for a long time, also due to system limitations (e.g. due to the fact that only the unemployed were entitled to the benefit or due to the obligation to undergo training).
7. Obtaining a social benefit is often associated with the fulfilment of several conditions — also the administrative procedures were often unnecessarily multiplied. People receiving benefits did not obtain sufficient support in finding work or motivation to improve their qualifications. Hence, only a small percentage of these individuals expressed readiness to work or participate in training.
8. In each of the Member States a certain percentage of individuals receiving social benefits while actively participating in the labour market could be seen — in Sweden it is about half of the beneficiaries (including 20% of those working full-time), 13% in France, Finland and the Netherlands, 8% in Luxembourg, about 7% in Germany and more than 5% in Portugal.
9. The Member States are looking for ways to improve these indicators through better targeting of limited resources to groups who need such support most.

10. Strong competition and the lack of basic skills means that there was no interest in general training. The design of training programs should help in filling the educational gaps and increasing employment opportunities.

Other European Union projects aimed at promoting employment and social inclusion include, among others [e.g. Szarfenberg 2009, p. 7–11]:

— the Community Charter of Fundamental Social Rights of Workers of 1989;
— the establishment of the Charter of Fundamental Rights in 2000;
— the adoption of the Lisbon Strategy in 2000;
— the establishment of the European Employment Strategy in 2007;
— the EQUAL Community Initiative completed in 2008, financed by the European Social Fund;
— the Recommendation of the Commission on the active inclusion of people excluded from the labour market (2008).

The European Anti-Poverty Network (EAPN) accepted the task of evaluating national plans for social inclusion. [Duffy 2002] The results of this evaluation are presented in the table below.

Table 46. EAPN Networks' view of the strengths and weaknesses of the NAPsincl29 process (up until July 2002)

	STRENGHTS	AREAS NEEDING IMPROVEMENT
1	First Treaty basis for combating poverty and exclusion	The NAPs/incl process may be a substitute for a legal framework rather than a means of developing a better legal framework
2	Peer review process amongst governments	There are no penalties if governments do not do what they say — except 'name and shame'
3	10 year horizon — so there is time to develop the content of the Plans and evaluate the impact of the Plans	So far, the networks have not seen any vision in the Plans
4	The four Objectives commonly agreed by governments mean that it should be simpler to compare and contrast national policies and therefore learn from best practice	Governments have interpreted the Objectives quite differently. Indicators are rather under-developed and usually quantitative. While the addition of some qualitative indicators may be seen as less 'objective', they may be also less easy for governments to manipulate
5	The four Objectives can form the basis of a comprehensive anti-poverty and exclusion Plan	Most governments have placed too much emphasis on access to work (especially 'workfare' type schemes) and given too little attention to rights,

---

[29] National Action Plans on Inclusion (author's note).

		inequality and public services accessible to all
6	The fourth Objective of mobilising all actors/bodies means the Plans have the potential to be national (not only government) Plans. The fourth Objective also provides scope to develop participatory processes in realising the Plans	So far, governments have paid little attention to this Objective — there are neither targets nor indicators and there is no proposal for structured and ongoing mobilisation of all bodies
7	The NAPs/incl are action Plans and strategies, not merely reports	Those Networks in countries with existing national anti-poverty strategies reported a lack of clarity in the relationship between NAPs/incl and these existing national strategies. There seems to be no significant cash or human resources dedicated to ensure realisation of the four Objectives governments have signed up to. Unlike the Employment Plans, there is no dedicated European financial instrument such as the Structural Funds.
8	There are cross-cutting themes that provide scope for dealing with inequities between groups	Gender issues were not consistently considered in the first reports and very little attention was paid to racial equality. There is not much evidence so far that the next Plans will be an improvement.
9	The presentation of best practice examples enhances opportunities for international learning	The basis for choosing the examples offered was not clear and most initiatives were government led. Thus the scope for learning is limited as between national governments and there is almost no scope for learning by civil society or other stakeholders
10	The extension of the process to 'accession' countries provides a real focus for anti-poverty and exclusion strategy amongst the more technical 'acquis'	Networks have concerns about the privatisation of social policies in certain applicant countries as part of the transition process. In addition, in the context of the NAPs/incl process, mobilising all actors would be a real challenge in some applicant countries

Source: [Duffy, p. 25].

In 2013, EAPN reassessed the National Reform Programmes. The purpose of the report was determining to what extent these programs pursued social objectives, related mainly to poverty, but also to employment and education. Based on the responses received from 19 Member States general conclusions were formulated (see Table 47).

Table 47. General assessment of the NPRs – key agreements

75% says that their respective NRP refers mostly to macroeconomic and financial management.
67% says that the opinion of the social and anti-poverty NGOs was not asked, nor taken seriously into account, by the government.
58% says that EAPN networks sent their proposal, comments and contributions to the national authorities, getting little or no influence on the outcome.
58% says that the poverty target "is not there" or "that there are few social measures beyond employment policies".
0% says that the NRP progresses towards an integrated strategy to fight poverty and social exclusion.

Source: [EAPN 2013, p.13].

Specific conclusions concerning combating poverty and social exclusion are not optimistic. It was stated that the objective of the fight against poverty has not been taken seriously — the lack of transparency and analysis of relevant indicators does not allow for defining the priorities in this area adequately. Both the EU strategy and the national strategies integrated with it should be equally important for all members, if the goal of social inclusion is to be achieved. Social investments that can play a key role are needed here. Some progress has been noticed in the implementation of the thematic priorities (such as child poverty or homelessness) but progress in the growth of employment, as a primary source of social inclusion, is still insufficient. [EAPN 2013, p. 9] The report also formulated recommendations for the implementation of the Europe 2020 strategy [EAPN 2013, p. 10]:

"1. Develop a Social Pact and Social Governance in the European Semester.
2. Immediate action to restrict austerity and promote social investment.
3. Integrated multi-dimensional strategy to fight poverty, based on access to rights, resources and services.
4. Targeted use of EU funds to reduce poverty and exclusion and support community-led and grass-root initiatives.
5. Radical reform of the Semester process, based on democratic and participative engagement and accountability."

The results presented in the report [Directorate-General Employment, Social Affairs and Equal Opportunities 2010] indicate that in the opinion of Europeans, the problem of poverty and social exclusion is common in their countries. Respondents also noted the increase in poverty over the past three years, due probably to the onset of the financial crisis, which has affected many countries. It was also found that the increase in poverty is largely due to lack of training or education, insufficient qualifications or hereditary poverty.

The rationale for including objectives relating to social inclusion in the Europe 2020 Strategy were previous experiences, earlier initiatives and demographic projections. Today, most European countries are, unfortunately, far from going on the path enabling them to achieve the objectives set in the strategy. This situation is caused by the recent economic crisis, which negatively influenced also the social welfare systems. As the statistical research shows [Poverty and social exclusion; http://ec.europa.eu/social/main.jsp?catId=751&langId=en]:

— 24% of the total EU population (120 million people) is at risk of poverty or social exclusion — this includes 27% of all children in Europe, 20.5% of people over 65 years, and 9% of the labour force;
— nearly 9% of Europeans are in a difficult financial situation; they often do not have such (seemingly basic in the 21st century) equipment as a telephone, a washing machine or a car, while lacking funds for heating their home or financing unexpected expenses;
— 17% of Europeans live on less than 60% of the median household income in their country;
— 10% of Europeans live in households where nobody has a job; 12 million more women than men live in poverty in the EU;
— social exclusion also often affects ethnic or social groups, such as the Roma, among which two thirds of people are unemployed, only every second child attends a nursery and only 15% of young people attend school.

Large disparities in the efficiency of social protection systems in different European countries were also noted — in the weakest ones, the risk of exclusion has been reduced by 15%, whereas in the most efficient ones by about 35%.

One of the Europe 2020 Strategy priorities is: "inclusive growth: fostering a high-employment economy delivering social and territorial cohesion". [European Commission 2010, p. 5] The objectives of the European Union, which should be implemented by it to ensure the implementation of the strategy, have been formulated as follows:

— 75% employment rate for women and men aged 20–64 by 2020 — achieved by getting more people into work, especially women, the young, older and the low-skilled, as well as legal immigrants;
— better educational attainment — in particular:
  - reducing school drop-out rates below 10%;
  - at least 40% of 30–34–year-olds completing third level education (or equivalent);

— at least 20 million fewer people in or at risk of poverty and social exclusion [European Commission 2010, p. 5].

In accordance with the recommendation of the European Commission on the active inclusion [Commission Recommendation 2008] in the 2014–2020 programming perspective the implementation of programmes aimed at promoting social inclusion and fighting poverty was foreseen [see e.g. European Commission 2011]. The planned basic pillars of the active inclusion system are the guaranteed minimum income, inclusive labour market and high quality integration services. In Poland, the European Social Fund is to finance one of the six operational programmes: *The Operational Programme "Knowledge, Education, Development"*, highlighting the following areas of support for individuals and communities, as well as for systems and structures:

9.4 Active integration, in particular to improve the employability;

9.6 Combating discrimination based on sex, race, ethnic origin or beliefs, disability, age or sexual orientation;

9.7 Facilitating access to affordable, sustainable and high quality services, including health care and social services for the general public;

9.8 Promoting the social economy and social enterprises.

The Regional Operational Programmes can support individuals and communities through funding obtained:

1. from the *European Regional Development Fund* in the following areas:

9.1 investments in infrastructure and social care, which will contribute to national, regional and local development, reducing inequalities in health status and transition from institutional to community level services;

9.2 supporting the physical, economic and social revitalization communities and poor urban and rural areas;

9.3 supporting social entrepreneurship;

2. from the *European Social Fund* to finance local development strategies implemented by communities (priority 9.9).

In 2013, the European Commission called on Member States to set priorities in the area of social investments and reform of social protection systems. The possibilities of financing the necessary actions from the European Social Fund for the years 2014–2020 were also indicated. [European Community 2013] The Communication presented the policy framework and the specific tasks that should be implemented by the European Union countries.

A package related to social investments was developed based on analysis of the data related to employment and social issues, as well as good practices. It was found that in Member States with a developed system of social investments a lower proportion of the population is at risk of social exclusion or poverty. The package takes into account the social, economic and budgetary differences between countries. The basic policy framework has been formulated as follows:

— the social security system should meet the needs of citizens in critical moments - this way higher social spending in the future can be avoided;
— the social policy should be simplified and better targeted, so as to allocate the available resources more precisely;
— there is a need to improve the strategy of active inclusion by ensuring affordable but also high-quality childcare and education to prevent early school leaving by children and young people or contribute to increasing the economic activity of their parents.

The available statistical data confirm the increase in unemployment in nearly all Member States, which also increases the risk of social exclusion and poverty (see Figure 26 and Figure 27). This situation jeopardizes the objectives of the 2020 strategy. There has also been an increase in disparity between northern and southern European countries. It was stressed that the limitations on social exclusion and poverty is significantly affected by the efficiency of spending, being a result of the general concept of the social system.

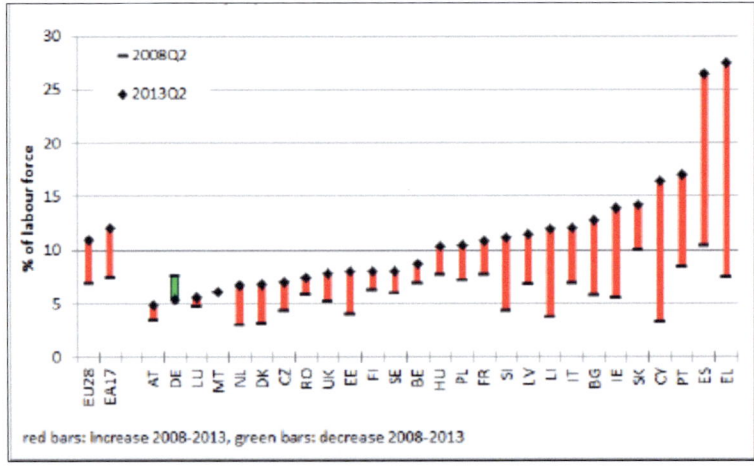

Figure 26. Unemployment rates across EU Members States
Source: [European Commission 2013, Special Edition].

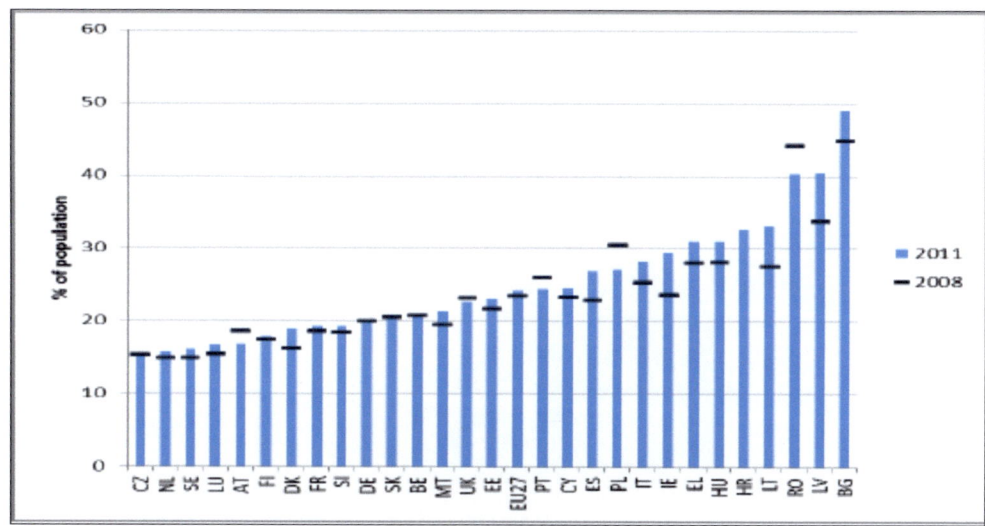

Figure 27. The risk of poverty and social exclusion
Source: [European Commission 2013,Special Edition].

In order to achieve the objectives of social inclusion established in the Europe 2020 strategy, it is important to detect the adverse trends in employment and social affairs at an early stage, as well as monitor the policies in these areas. Preparing effective actions and the exchange of best practices to promote convergence will then become possible. While the procedure related to the macroeconomic imbalances was developed and introduced in 2011, it has been neglecting the social issues so far. In order to recognize the social impact, supplementing the already monitored unemployment rate with other indicators from the field of employment and social affairs was proposed. Such indicators may include:

— the participation rate in the labour market;
— the long-term unemployment rate;
— the unemployment rate among young people (including young people who are not employed and not in education or training);
— the rate of "risk of poverty and social exclusion" (supplemented by three supporting indicators: an indicator of the risk of poverty, extreme material deprivation indicator and the percentage of people living in households with low work intensity) [EU COM 2013, 690, p. 4–5].

The indicators related to social exclusion and poverty are monitored in the European Union by different organizations. In 2013 the latest report was published, containing also statistical data on social protection, demographic trends or income and living conditions [European Social Statistics 2013]. A synthetic indicator allowing for the assessment the risks of exclusion was also proposed.[30] It was found that in 2011 there were more than 119 million people at the risk of exclusion or poverty according to at least one of the criteria, which represents about 24% of the total EU population (see Figure 28).

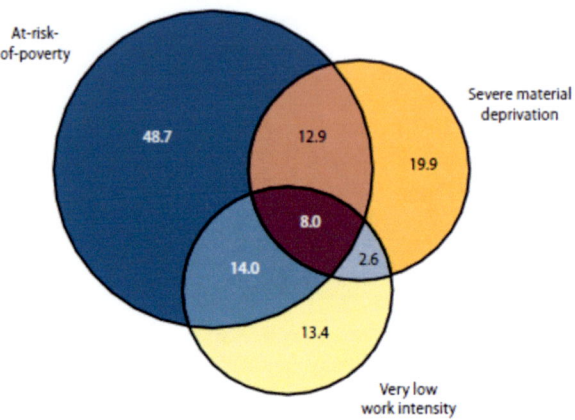

Figure 28. Number of people at risk of poverty or social exclusion analysed by type of risks (EU-27)
Source: [Social Statistics Report 2013, p. 171].

Although a decrease in the number of people at risk of exclusion or poverty in 2005–2009 was observed, since 2010 this trend has been reversed. Significant differences in the individual countries are also visible: in the Czech Republic the share of people at risk of exclusion or poverty in 2011 was 15.3%, while in Bulgaria there were as much

---

[30] This rate is defined as follow: „The at-risk-of-poverty rate is the share of persons with an equivalised disposable income (after social transfers) below the at-risk-of-poverty threshold, which is set at 60 % of the national median equivalised disposable income after social transfers. This indicator does not measure wealth or poverty, but low income in comparison with other residents in that country, which does not necessarily imply a low standard of living. The at-risk-of-poverty rate before social transfers is calculated as the share of persons having an equivalised disposable income before social transfers that is below the at-risk-of-poverty threshold calculated after social transfers. Pensions, such as old age and survivors' (widows' and widowers') benefits, are counted as income (social transfers) and not as social transfers. This indicator examines the hypothetical nonexistence of social transfers" [European Social Statistics 2013, p. 214].

as 49.1% of them. [Social Statistics Report 2013, p. 170] The analysis of the data on the risk of social exclusion in the countries of the Baltic Sea Region leads to the conclusion that in most countries the risk has slightly decreased, while in Denmark, Estonia and Sweden, this ratio has increased (see Table 48).

Table 48. People at risk of poverty or social exclusion (% of total population) in BSR countries

Country/ year	2005	2006	2007	2008	2009	2010	2011	2012
EU27	25.6	25.2	24.4	23.6	23.1	23.6	24.2	24.8
DK	17.2	16.7	16.8	16.3	17.6	18.3	18.9	19
EE	25.9	22	22	21.8	23.4	21.7	23.1	23.4
FI	17.2	17.1	17.4	17.4	16.9	16.9	17.9	17.2
DE	18.4	20.2	20.6	20.1	20	19.7	19.9	19.6
LV	45.8	41.4	36	33.8	37.4	38.1	40.4	36.6
LT	41	35.9	28.7	27.6	29.5	33.4	33.4	32.5
NO	16.2	16.9	16.5	15	15.2	14.9	14.6	13.8
PL	45.3	39.5	34.4	30.5	27.8	27.8	27.2	26.7
SE	14.4	16.3	13.9	14.9	15.9	15	16.1	18.2

Source: own, based on Eurostat.

The EU's expenditure on social protection in 2010 accounted for about 29% of its Gross Domestic Product (GDP). Among the Baltic countries, the highest level of social protection expenditure was recorded in Denmark, Germany and Sweden (over 30%), while in Poland, Lithuania, Latvia and Estonia these expenditures accounted for less than 20% of GDP. [Social Statistics Report 2013, p. 198] The beneficiaries of social security were mostly elderly, sick or disabled (see Figure 29).

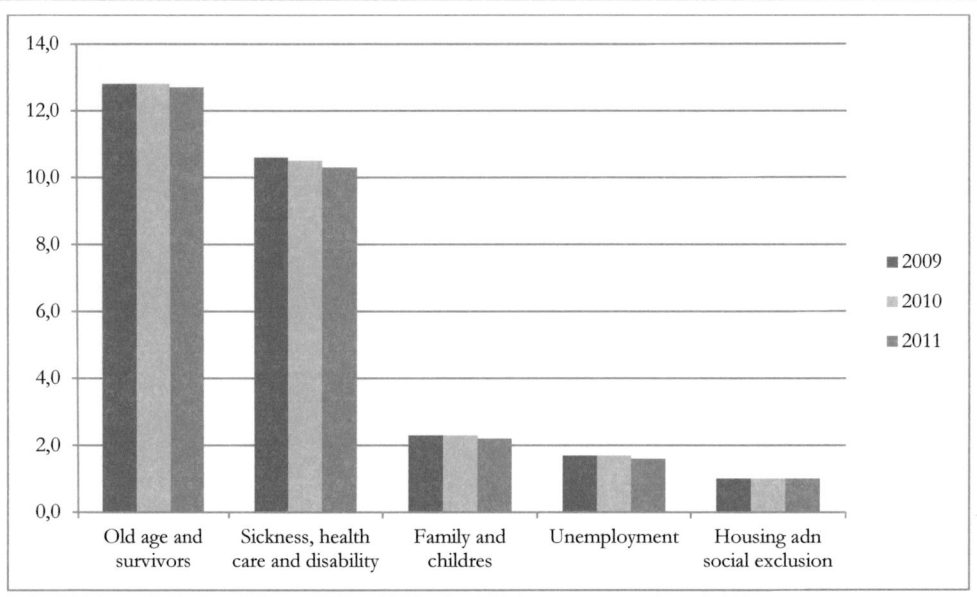

Figure 29. Social protection benefits by groups of functions in 2009-2011 as a % of GDP (EU-27)
Source: own, based on Eurostat

In a report prepared by the Directorate-General Employment, Social Affairs and Inclusion for the European Commission, the results of the social climate were presented. [Directorate-General Employment, Social Affairs and Inclusion 2012] The index of the social climate of the European Union takes into account the assessments of the individual factors (personal circumstances), providing a reflection of the national social protection and social inclusion policy.[31] The average value of the index in the EU in 2012 is slightly lower than in 2009–2011. It is interesting that men assessed the social climate higher than women. In contrast, after comparing the results in the different countries it was observed that the social climate had improved in many of them — the most significant increase among the BSR countries was recorded in Germany and Sweden. In turn, the assessment of the social climate in other countries is rather negative (e.g. in Poland in 2012 the index value was -2.6 and in Lithuania it amounted to -2.4). Compared with the year 2011, the most significant increase in the

---

[31] "A neutral index is an index score close to 0 on a scale from -10 to 10, meaning that respondent perception on an item is neither positive nor negative." [Directorate-General Employment, Social Affairs and Inclusion 2012, footnote p. 4].

index value was recorded in Lithuania (0.5) and Latvia (0.8). In contrast, the index dropped significantly in Poland (1.3 compared to 2009).

Table 49. Overall Social Climate Index in BSR countries

Country/ year	2009	2010	2011	2012
EU27	-0.7	-0.7	-0.6	-0.8
DK	2.8	2.4	2.1	2.8
EE	-0.4	0	-0.3	-0.4
FI	1.4	1.4	1.1	1.5
DE	0.3	0.7	1.4	2
LV	-2.2	-2.3	-2.7	-1.9
LT	-2.5	-3.1	-2.9	-2.4
PL	-1.3	-1.4	-1.7	-2.6
SE	1.8	2.3	2.2	2.6

Source: [Directorate-General Employment, Social Affairs and Inclusion 2012, p. 8].

The assessment of policy and social climate is a derivative of the assessment of the economic situation. As noted in subsequent studies, more than two thirds of Europeans perceive the economic situation in their country as poor, although clear differences in the assessment of individual countries can be seen [European Commission 2013, p. 18].

Table 50. Overall Social Climate Index in BSR countries

Country/ perception	total "good"	total "bad"	"don't know"
EU28	68%	31%	1%
DK	74%	24%	2%
EE	44%	54%	2%
FI	47%	53%	0%
DE	82%	16%	2%
LV	21%	77%	2%
LT	27%	70%	3%
PL	35%	61%	4%
SE	85%	14%	1%

Source: own, based on [European Commission 2013c, p. 17–20].

Compared to the research carried out in spring 2013, the assessment of the economic situation has improved in most BSR countries, with the exception of Lithuania and Finland. [European Commission 2013, p. 19–20]

In the report showing the social progress[32] [Porter, Stern, Artavia Loria 2013, p. 8] it was concluded that:

— "Economic development is necessary but not sufficient for social progress.
— A country's overall level of development masks social and environmental strengths and challenges.
— At a disaggregated level, the Social Progress Index shows areas of underperformance and success for countries at all income levels."

The social progress indicator is calculated on the basis of the following five characteristics:

— Based exclusively on non-economic indicators.
— Based exclusively on outcome indicators.
— Integrates a large number of indicators into an aggregate score of social progress.
— Model is structured to allow empirical investigation of relationships between dimensions, components and indicators.
— Breadth of indicators makes the model relevant for countries at all income levels.

The structure of this indicator is presented in the figure 30.

Among the presented fifty countries, the highest value of the ratio was noted in Sweden, Germany is in the 5th place, whereas Poland in the 13th [Porter, Stern, Artavia Loria 2013, p. 8]. It should be remembered that social progress depends on political decisions, investments, implementation capacities and the cooperation of interested parties (both administration and societies or business).

Two leading initiatives are to be conducive to the achievement of the social objectives defined in the Europe 2020 strategy: the Innovation Union and the European Platform against Poverty and Social Exclusion. In addition, many opportunities to develop and implement social innovation will come with the launch of the Horizon 2020 research and innovation programme.

The results of the social climate research confirm that despite many efforts and programmes aimed at disadvantaged groups, much remains to be done, as in many coun-

---

[32] "social progress is the capacity of a society to meet the basic human needs of its citizens, establish the building blocks that allow citizens and communities to enhance and sustain the quality of their lives, and create the conditions for all individuals to reach their full potential" [Porter, Stern, Artavia Loria 2013, p. 7].

tries the situation in this area has deteriorated. It is fundamental to identify and select the right tools, which can be specific for given countries or social groups.

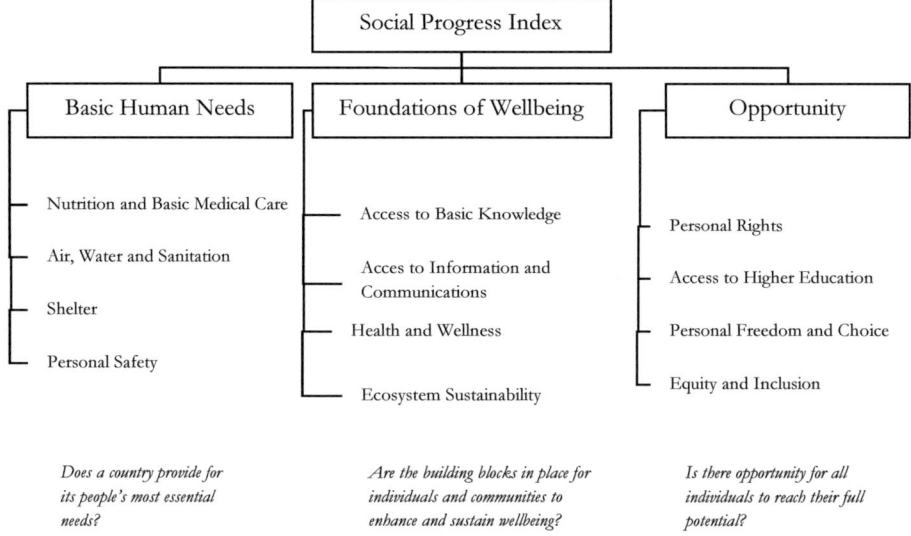

Figure 30. Structure the Social Progress Index
Source: [Porter, Stern, Artavia Loria 2013, p. 8].

5. 3. Women's activity – why not? - entrepreneurship and innovativeness of women

Entrepreneurship is often seen as a factor conducive to economic growth due to stimulating innovation, competition and industry dynamics. On the other hand, entrepreneurship is a complex phenomenon involving many participants and requires a multilevel analysis. Therefore, the early stage of entrepreneurial activity (creating and running one's own business) or manifestations of employee enterprise — the intrapreneurship — can be examined. As the results of various studies show, women's participation in entrepreneurship varies greatly in different countries. Attention is also paid to women as a group which is often disadvantaged in the labour market. For example, female single parents are one of the disadvantaged groups in the labour market. Due to their need to adapt their daily timetable to the opening hours of public institutions (schools, kindergartens, nurseries), they are less attractive candidates for employees. An additional obstacle is often their lack of education and low skills. Activities aimed at increasing the economic activity of these women may include trainings or courses enabling them to raise their professional qualifications or make their working hours more flexible, or even work partly from home.

As the statistical data show, women are often better educated than men (see Table 51), but among entrepreneurs there are more men than women (see Figure 31 and 32). Typically, women employed in the same positions as men earn on average about 15% less [Entrepreneurship at a Glance 2012 and 2013].

Table 51. Women among students in ISCED 5-6 - as % of the total students at this level in BSR countries

	2002	2003	2004	2005	2006	2007	2008	2009	2010	2011
EU27	54.4	54.5	54.8	54.9	55.1	55.2	55.3	55.5	55.4	55.2
DK	57.5	57.9	57.9	57.4	57.4	57.6	58.0	58.2	58.1	57.6
EE	61.5	61.5	61.8	61.5	61.6	61.1	61.7	61.9	60.9	59.7
FI	54.1	53.5	53.4	53.6	53.9	54.0	54.2	54.0	53.8	54.0
DE	49.0	49.5	49.4	49.6	49.7	49.7	49.7	51.4	51.3	50.6
LV	61.5	61.7	62.3	63.2	63.3	63.9	64.4	63.7	62.7	61.1
LT	60.5	60.0	60.0	60.1	59.9	60.0	59.9	59.2	59.4	59.0
NO	59.6	59.7	59.6	59.6	59.7	60.2	60.8	61.1	60.8	60.3
PL	57.9	57.8	57.6	57.5	57.4	57.4	57.6	57.9	59.2	59.9
SE	59.5	59.6	59.6	59.6	59.6	59.9	60.3	60.1	59.4	59.1

Source: [Eurostat 2013, http://appsso.eurostat.ec.europa.eu/nui/submitViewTable
Acion.do;jsessionid=9ea7d07e30da1c698dd3699d4673b3b8f7523d1ca0dc.e34MbxeSahmMa4
0LbNiMbxaMc34Oe0].

It could be noticed that women constitute a majority of students at tertiary level of education. Only in Germany in the early twenty-first century men predominated among students, however since 2009 also here the percentage of female students has begun to be higher than the percentage of male students. In most countries of the Baltic Sea Region the percentage of female students was higher than the EU average. The exceptions are Germany and Finland.

In addition to the level of education, the direction of education is also important: more women than men study education, health and welfare and humanities & arts. In contrast, far fewer women than men study science majors, such as mathematics, computing, engineering, manufacturing or construction. The percentage of women studying social science, business and law fields is higher than the EU average in most countries of the Baltic Sea Region with the exception of Germany [see Eurostat data or the European Social Statistics 2013, p. 112]. Education for entrepreneurship translates into later professional activity or participation in the labour market, although the relevance of education in different countries varies greatly. The statistical data show that enterprises are started more often by men than by women. The highest rates of self-employment among the BSR countries were observed in Poland — it may be related to employers' forcing their contractors to establish sole proprietorships to reduce costs (see Figure 31).

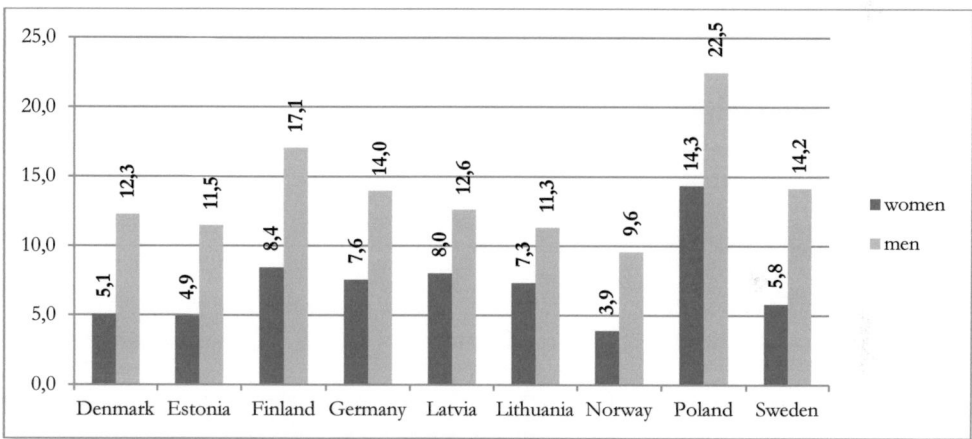

Figure 31. Share of self-employment men and women in BSR countries (%, in 2011)
Source: own base on *Entrepreneurship at a Glance* 2013.

A significantly lower participation rates of men and women as employers were also observed, and the rate for men is three times higher than for women (see: Figure 5.7).

The report [Entrepreneurship at a Glance 2013, p. 66] highlighted the importance of women's entrepreneurship as a key source of innovation and new jobs. At the same time attention was drawn to the difficulties in measuring the impact of gender on entrepreneurial attitudes and orienting adequate tools towards supporting the participation of women in this field. It is also important to monitor the activities of enterprising men and women depending on the business cycle.

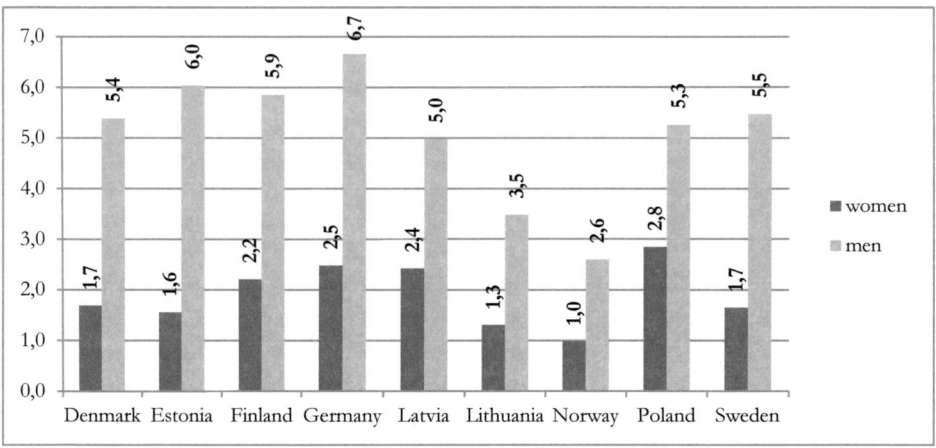

Figure 32. Share of men and women employers in BSR countries (%, in 2011)
Source: own, based on *Entrepreneurship at a Glance* 2013.

The results of research on entrepreneurship presented in the Global Entrepreneurship Monitor report [GEM 2012 GEM 2013 GEM Women 2013] indicate significant differences in entrepreneurship of women and men. The research also takes into account the differences in the economic development of individual countries[33]. The Baltic Sea Region countries were classified as follows:

— developing and efficiency driven economy: Estonia, Latvia, Lithuania and Poland;
— developed and innovation driven: Denmark, Finland, Germany, Sweden and Norway.

Much more frequent motives for taking up entrepreneurial activity in all the BSR countries were the opportunities perceived in the environment, whereas the pure necessity was rarer. In Poland, Sweden and Lithuania women were more likely than men to start their own business out of necessity — however, they were also better at

---

[33] The worlds' economies were categorized into three groups: factor, efficiency and innovation driven. Moreover, the developing and developed economies were distinguished.

perceiving the opportunities (see Figure 33). Women also feared the collapse of their enterprises definitely more often, despite the perceived potential opportunities to develop them [Kelley, Brush, Greene 2013].

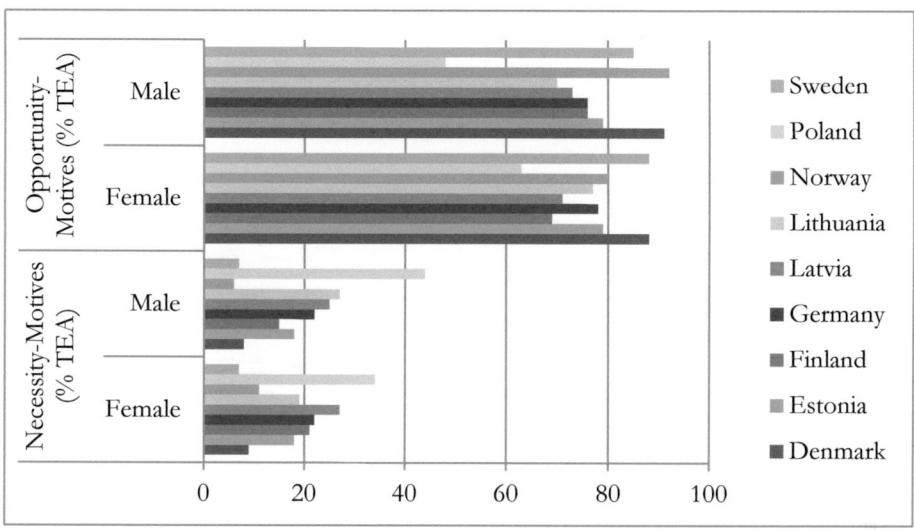

Figure 33. Necessity and Opportunity Motives for Women and Men Entrepreneurs (TEA34)
Source: own base on [Kelley, Brush., Greene 2013].

---

[34] TEA is a Total Entrepreneurial Activity (see Global Entrepreneurship Monitor; author' note).

Table 52. Key Activity and Profile Indicators for Women and Men

	Total Entrepreneurship Activity (TEA) % of adult population		Established Business Ownership Rate % of adult population		Discontinuing a Business in the Past Year (% Adult Population)		At Least a Post-Secondary Degree (% TEA)		Businesses Have One Founder (% TEA)	
	Female	Male	Female	Male	Female	Male	Female	Male	Female	Male
DK	3	8	2	5	6	5	84	71	58	51
EE	10	19	4	11	2	6	59	35	35	38
FI	4	8	4	12	2	0	55	32	64	44
DE	4	7	4	6	2	10	58	43	66	46
LV	8	19	6	10	6	6	63	46	43	48
LT	4	9	4	12	0	1	86	61	58	47
PL	6	13	3	8	7	4	31	22	75	69
SE	5	8	3	7	7	4	61	37	53	59
NO	4	10	4	8	6	5	66	50	54	51

Source: own base on [Kelley, Brush, Greene 2013].

The results also confirm that in developed Europe innovation levels for women entrepreneurs are high (32%) and equal to that of men. In European developing countries, on the other hand, this ratio does not exceed 25% for both genders. However, women are far less likely than men to expect the growth of their enterprise, although in the European developing countries ¼ of women entrepreneurs expect to employ at least five new workers in the next five years.

It has to be remembered that economic growth and condition of any economy is heavily dependent on the dynamics of entrepreneurship, regardless of the stage of development or region. In order to stimulate activity in this area properly motivated and skilled people are needed — individuals who will be starting enterprises and developing them. On the other hand, these people should be provided with adequate conditions for doing business — created both by the public and by the administration. Research on women's entrepreneurship, and especially the motives behind their taking up activity, can be a valuable source of information for individuals and organizations involved in the implementation and attainment of the objectives of the Europe 2020 strategy in the area of entrepreneurship, employment and innovation.

References

1. Andersen, J., Bruto da Costa, A., Chigot, C., Duffy, K., Mancho, S., Mernagh, M. (1994), *The contribution of Poverty 3 to the understanding of poverty, exclusion and integration,* in: *Poverty 3: The Lessons of the Poverty 3 Programme,* European Economic Interest Group, Animation and Research, Lille.
2. Atkinson A.B., Hills J. (1998*), Exclusion, Employment and Opportunity,* Centre of Anaysis of Social Exclusion, London School of Economics, London.
3. Collins H. (2003), *Discrimination, Equality and Social Inclusion,* The Modern Law Review, vol. 66, p.16-43.
4. *Commission Recommendation on the active inclusion of people excluded from the labour market* (2008), Official Journal of the European Union L307, 3.10.2008 P. 11-14.
5. *Council Decision of 18 July 1989 establishing a medium -term Community action programme concerning the economic and social integration of the economically and socially less privileged groups in society,* Official Journal of the European Union L 224 , 02/08/1989, (89/457/EEC).
6. *Council Decision of 19 December 1984 on specific Community action to combat poverty,* Official Journal of the European Union L 002 , 03/01/1985 P. 0024 – 0025, (85/8/EEC).
7. *Council Recommendation of 24 June 1992 on common criteria concerning sufficient resources and social assistance in social protection systems,* Official Journal of the European Union L 245, 26.08.1992 P. 0046 – 0048, (92/441/EEC), Brussels.
8. *Council Recommendation of 27 July 1992 on the convergence of social protection objectives and policies,* Official Journal of the European Union L 245 , 26.08.1992 P. 0049 – 0052, (92/442/EEC), Brussels.
9. Directorate-General Employment, Social Affairs and Equal Opportunities (2010), *Poverty and Social Exclusion. Report,* Special Eurobarometer 355.
10. Directorate-General Employment, Social Affairs and Inclusion (2012), *Social climante,* Special Eurobarometer 391.
11. Duffy K. (2002), *EAPN follow up on the National Plans on Inclusion. The state of play by June 2002,* EAPN, Brussels.
12. EAPN (2013), *Widening the Gap. EAPN Assesment of the National Reform programmes 2013,* Brussels.
13. European Commision (2008), *Recommendation on the active inclusion of pewple excluded from the labour market,* Official Journal of the European Union L 307, 18.11.2008 p. 11-14, Brussels, (2008/867/EC).
14. European Commision (2011), P*roposal for a regulation of the Europrean Parliament and the Council on on specific provisions concerning the European Regional Development Fund and the Investment for growth and jobs goal and repealing Regulation,* (EC) No 1080/2006h, Brussels, 6.10.2011, COM(2011) 614 final.

15. European Commision, Communication (2005), *Pracując razem, pracując lepiej: Nowe ramy otwartej koordynacji polityk ochrony socjalnej i integracji społecznej w Unii Europejskiej*, COM(2005) 706, 22.12.2005.

16. European Commision, Communication (2010), *A strategy for smart, sustainable and inclusive growth*, Brussels, 3.03.2010, COM(2010) 2020 final.

17. European Commision, Communication (2013a), *Strenghthening the social dimension of the economic and monetary union*, Brussels, 2.10.2013, COM(2013) 690 provisoire.

18. European Commission (2013b), *EU Employment and Social Situation*, Special Edition: Annual Overiew September 2013.

19. European Commission staff working document (2010), *Joint Report on Social Protection and Social Inclusion*, COM(2010) final, Brussels.

20. European Commission staff working document (2013), *Social investment through the European Social Fund*, SWD (2013) 44 final, Brussels.

21. European Community (2013), *Public opinion in the European Union. First results*, Standard Eurobarometer 80.

22. European Community, *Report from the Commission on the implementation od the recommendation 92/441/EEc of 24 June 1992 on common criteria concerning sufficient resources and social assistance in social protection systems*, Brussels, 25.01.1999, COM(1998) 774 final.

23. *European Social Statistics* (2013), Eurostat, Luxembourg.

24. Eurostat (2013) [http://appsso.eurostat.ec.europa.eu/nui/submitViewTable Acion.do;jsessionid=9ea7d07e30da1c698dd3699d4673b3b8f7523d1ca0dc.e34Mbx eSahmMa40LbNiMbxaMc34Oe0 access: 20-12-2013].

25. Fairlie R.W. (2013), *Entrepreneurial activity 1996-2012*, Ewing Marion Kaufmann Foundation.

26. Kelley D. J., Brush C. G., Greene P. G., Litovsky Y. (2013), *Global Entrepreneurship Monitor 2012 Women's Report*, Babson College in Wellesley, Massachusetts.

27. Xavier R., Kelley D.J., Kew J., Herrington M., Vorderwülbecke A. (2013), *The Global Entreprenership Monitor 2012 Global Report*, Global Entrepreneurship Research Association.

28. Kelley D.J., Singer S., Herrington M. (2012), *The Global Entreprenership Monitor*, Global Entrepreneurship Research Association.

29. Muras M., Ivanov A. (red.) (2006), *Wykluczenie i integracja społeczna w Polsce. Ujęcie wskaźnikowe*, Ministerstwo Pracy i Polityki Społecznej, Warszawa.

30. OECD (2012), *Entrepreneurship at a Glance*, OECD Publishing.

31. OECD (2013), *Entrepreneurship at a Glance*, OECD Publishing.

32. Porter M.E., Stern S, Artavia Loria R. (2013), *Social Progress Index 2013*, Social Progress Imperative, Washington DC.

33. *Proposal of the European Commmmission on establishing a medium-term action programme to combat exclusion and promote solidarity: a new programme to support and stimulate innovation (1994-1999)* (COM (93) 435 (not published in the Official Journal).

34. Resolution of the Council of 21 January 1974 concerning a social action programme, *Social action programme*, Bulletin of the European Communities, Suplement 2/74.

35. Rusin M., Sobolewska K., Bujko J. (2010), *Diagnoza osób defaworyzowanych na rynku pracy*, Wałbrzych.

36. Silver, H. (1995), *Reconceptualizing social disadvantage: Three paradigms of social exclusion*, in: G. Rogers, Ch. Gore, J.B. Figueiredo (ed.) *Social Exclusion: Rhetoric Reality Responses*, International Institute for Labou Studies, International Labour Organization, Geneva.

Chapter VI Examples of good practice in building competitiveness

6. 1. Possibilities and conditions of good practice transfer

Adaptation of solutions used in one organization to the needs of another is usually implemented using the concept of benchmarking. However, it should not be equated with imitation. It consists rather in learning from others than in copying solutions. The use of benchmarking requires very broad knowledge allowing not only for assessment of an organization, but also for finding ways to improve its functioning in another organization. It is often necessary to adapt the identified practices to the specificity of the follower organization. The process of benchmarking is therefore composed of a number of efforts in identifying, studying, analysing and adapting good practices and their results. Implementation of good practice in an organization should provide added value. As Harper suggests, [Harper 1996]: "Benchmarking provides the quantum leaps needed to keep on top".

Bogan and English [Bogan, English 1994] consider benchmarking to be an extremely useful strategic tool. It strengthens the process of planning and helps in strategic thinking. Benchmarking is more and more frequently used in the area of organizational strategy. Thanks to benchmarking enterprises can use internal or external resources in order to gain market leadership. Benchmarking helps to identify best practices in human resource management, which allows for developing the skills and qualifications of employees fully, and that may also contribute to the enterprise strategy. However, the successful implementation of a given solution depends on many factors, including the choice of an appropriate solution, determination of the effectiveness of its implementation and ensuring relevant conditions in the follower organization. It should also be kept in mind that the effects of the implementation of the borrowed solution in the area of management appear, at best, after a period of time, which may discourage organizations from this kind of activity. Benchmarking is also very time-consuming, although numerous examples of organizational practices constituting proof of the successful adaptation of someone else's solutions with one's own creative contribution can be found. Such databases are maintained e.g. by the International Benchmarking Clearinghouse, the Global Procurement and Supply Chain Electronic Benchmarking Network or the Best Practice LLC at the Harvard Business School. The Internet resources also provide numerous examples of good practice in different areas (e.g. http://www.unhabitat.org/content.asp?typeid=19&catid=34&cid=10256; http://www.zysk50plus.pl/?module=Default&action=ContentController&sectionId=6&parentId=6)

Therefore, while analysing the possibilities of implementing the solutions related to the activation of the seniors and women used in some countries to others, the national specificities and the cultural, organizational, financial or formal and legal background should certainly be taken into account. A more detailed analysis of the conditions of transfer of good practices described in the following sections can be found in a report prepared for the QUICK IGA project[35] [Grzesiak, Richert-Kaźmierska 2013].

6. 2. How to use the potential of seniors?

In the business practice of many countries, examples of good practice enabling the use of the potential of seniors through e.g. encouraging them to remain active in the labour market, can be found.

Such good practices have been identified during the implementation of the QUICK IGA project. The possibility of their transfer to the southern countries of the Baltic Sea Region are presented in the prepared reports. Some examples of good practice are presented below. The descriptions taken directly from the above-mentioned report [Grzesiak, Olczyk, Richert-Kaźmierska, Starnawska 2013].

6.2.1 Senior policy in working life

This practice was originally implemented in Norway by the Centre for Senior Policy. The aim of this initiative is to keep the elders as long as possible in labour market. The target group were workers from the age of 45 to 50.

Senior policy in working life is based on a strategy of cooperation between relevant government agencies, major unions, employer associations and other professionals. The aims, and the most essential means, are presented in National Initiative for Senior Workers in Norway and The Tripartite Agreement on a More Inclusive Workplace – a contract signed up by the government and social partners.

CSP is responsible for coordinating the National Initiative. The Initiative was implemented in order to discourage older workers from retiring early and promote a longer working career. The target group are workers from the age of 45–50. The Initiative is part of the strategy aimed at top management of all the major unions, employers' associations and relevant government agencies. In brief, the Initiative consists of the following elements:

---

[35] QUICK IGA – Innovative SMEs by Gender and Age; Part-financed by the European Union (European Development Fund and European Neighbourhood and Partnership Instrument.

— Promote awareness of the potentials and resources older employees hold.
— Provide a better and more inclusive working environment for all workers.
— Create more cooperation among labour, employer and government organizations and authorities concerning senior policy.

The Tripartite Agreement on a More Inclusive Workplace is an initiative supported by the Government and its social partners to encourage people with different hindrances for employment, such as disability, early retirement pension or sickness benefits, to return to work, at least part time. The agreement, which lasted from October 2001 to 31 December 2005, had three objectives, which match the intention of the senior policy:

— Reduce sick leave by at least 20% by the end of the agreement period.
— Significantly increase employment among those that have minor disabilities.
— Increase the average age at which seniors choose to retire.

The aim is to achieve these objectives through voluntary agreements between company-level employers and the National Insurance Authority, with CSP as an important coordinator. To this end, the Centre has worked out a national plan in cooperation with the social partners to make individuals, companies and politicians aware of the advantages of hiring and retaining workers over the age of 45.

The majority of the senior policy initiatives are focused on promoting good personnel policy in general and create a more accommodating workplace. Senior policy is based upon experiences that show that personnel policy initiatives and other developing methods must have a life span perspective. Preventive efforts must therefore begin early in a person's career.

6.2.2 Senior enterprises – experience never ages

This practice was originally implemented in Ireland by the Mid East Regional Authority. The initiative aims to people aged 50 + interested in starting their own business or those who are willing to provide advisory services to entrepreneurs aged 50 +. The target group were persons aged 50+ (employees, unemployed, economically inactive).

There are four main areas of the initiative:

— providing the knowledge and building the awareness - mainly training for people aged 50+ diagnosing and presenting the possibilities of their professional development, including starting the own business; distribution of information about tools available for new business owners – start-up's supporting system

— substantive and organizational support for those persons 50+ who decide to start their own business including assistance in finding partners (training, financial assistance, a database of potential business partners)
— maintain the database of individuals aged 50 + interested in investing their funds in new business (Business Angels)
— cooperation with people 50 +: entrepreneurs, professionals in various fields of business, interested in providing advisory services (mentoring) for new entrepreneurs, including those aged 50 + (group and individual meetings with counsellors).

Rising awareness' activities are addressed to three main target groups:

— those aged 50+ to present the possibilities given by the initiative;
— enterprise development agencies, financial institutions, agencies working with older people, younger entrepreneurs to show up the untapped potential that exists among older people;
— policy makers (politicians on different levels) to convince them to the idea of 50+ engagement in economy.

Starting and partnering activities deliver support instruments that help older persons to start their new business (by themselves or in partnership with younger ones). The initiative supports older individuals to explore the personal, financial and commercial aspects involved in taking the first step into entrepreneurship. Those aged 50+ may consider starting a business in partnership with a younger individual. The drive and enthusiasm of the younger person would then benefit from the wider knowledge, experience, networks and resources of the older individual.

Investing and acquiring, those are activities focused on "using" the finances of successful 50+, who represent an excellent potential source of investment. In many respects the most rewarding form of investment is when an individual aged 50+ invests in a business sector that he/she knows well and brings expertise, as well as money, to the new business (start-up).

Advising area is very important part of the initiative. Suitably qualified and experienced older people provide the support to owner managers of new and existing businesses. They share with their knowledge and experience with the younger and help them in designing strategic plans for their companies' development.

The initiative is supported by EU funds (INTERREG IVB NWE). It is run by The Senior Enterprise Association, which has a variety of membership categories including individuals and organizations from the public, private and NGO sectors and a very wide membership scope is encouraged. The lead partner is The Mid East Regional Authority but the initiative is also supported by the royal family. One of the partners is PRIME – The Prince's Initiative for Mature Enterprise.

6.2.3 Flexible work practices

This practice was originally implemented in Sweden by the Kronoberg County Council. The initiative tries to adopt the age-management approach by improving the ability of employees aged over 55 years to stay at work. The council wants to create a positive attitude among management in relation to its own and other employees' ageing. The initiative also aims to increase management's ability to create individual solutions that took into account older employees' strengths and weaknesses, and to develop a more person-focused leadership approach that would benefit all employees, irrespective of age. The target group were employees aged 55+.

The Kronoberg County Council's most important responsibility relates to health care, and around 85% of its activity is devoted to medical and health services. The council represents the largest employer in the county of Kronoberg, with 5,280 employees, 80% of whom are women. The five largest staff categories are nurses (28%), assistant nurses (15%), doctors (9%), keepers (9%) and administrators (8%). Employees' average age is 47 years. Almost 20% of the workforce are aged between 50 and 59 years, almost 28% are over 55 years and more than 11% are aged over 60 years. The council expects many employees to retire within 10 years. Staff turnover is currently 6.7%.

The main problem in personnel policy — it is recognized by the council is that 40% of health care employees will leave the labour market within 15 years. Therefore, the council depends on its older employees for both skills and staffing.

The presented initiative includes:

— skills training for managers – a plan for manager training is being prepared to ensure that the original initiative is implemented in everyday activities
— using pensioners as substitutes – employees at two of the council's facilities can continue to work as substitutes after retirement when they reach 64 years of age
— career planning at 55 years of age
— mentorship – one of the council's facilities has a structured skills-transfer programme
— enhancing workers' employability – the county council aims to keep all workers' skills up-to-date to preserve their employability

— learning centre – the council has set up local learning centres that use modern techniques and where workers can pursue formal education or other training, flexibly and at their own pace
— validation – the council plans to validate experience-based knowledge so that workers can more easily move between job categories or employers
— career and advice centre – the council plans to set up a career and advice centre to facilitate career planning.

6.2.4 Higher Vocational Education

This practice was originally implemented in Sweden by Sensus Study Association. This kind of educational action is addressed to professionals (employees) who are interested in upgrading their skills and developing their professional career. The target group were adults (35+) interested in upgrading their skills (average age of Sensus' students – 38 years old).

Higher vocational programme may be of 200 vocational credits (equivalent to one full academic year) or 400 vocational credits, corresponding to two full academic years.

The Swedish National Agency is responsible for allocation of funds to this type of education in Sweden.

Currently, there are 1100 courses like this in Sweden, realized by different types of educational organizations (Sensus runs only one course – International Key Account Manager).

Procedure of preparing the Higher Vocational Education Programme:

— steering group (different regional stakeholders, e.g. entrepreneurs, representatives of local authorities, representatives of trade unions etc.) execute an analysis of the regional labour market's situation, especially in the field of scarce occupations;
— teachers, coaches, mentors and trainers in the course – high level specialists, practitioners from different types of institutions;
— programme aim – formation of mainly practical high professional skills;
— educational organization interested in running such a course must apply for funds to Swedish National Agency – one application for two editions of the course;
— course group – 30–35 persons;
— courses last 2–4 semesters (10 hours of classes per week + own projects work + learning in work environment).

Higher Vocational Education Programme's result: more very highly qualified specialists, needed in regional labour market and ready to take over the managerial responsibilities.

6.2.5 Age management programme – Vattenfall AB

This practice was originally implemented in Sweden by Vatenfall AB, large firm form the energy branch. The target group were workers aged 57–65. Because of necessity of funds (due to the information from Scandinavian project' Partners) this initiative was not recommended for transfer. Within this initiative in Sweden the following activities were offered:

1. Organization of the personnel management – "cooperation council" which includes company managers and union representatives. This group has four main areas of activity:

— youth-related issues;
— age management;
— restructuring;
— skills development.
The group meets every three months and discusses all major issues within these categories.

2. The programme of age management, which has four overarching components:

— motivating the ageing workforce (series of '57+ seminars', 80/90/100 programme: employees can apply to work 80% of the hours for 90% of the wage and 100% of the pension contributions);
— skills transfer (seminars where participants are presented with texts illustrating situations and asking the senior employee to document their knowledge of how to deal with that situation);
— the establishment of an internal and external labour market for replacement/outplacement (Resource Management Centre);
— shaping internal opinion positively in favour of older workers
3. Age-conscious team management (composition of teams, where managers have started considering different mixes of older and younger workers in groups to make it easier for older workers by pairing them with younger, stronger workers who can do heavy lifting).

4. Preventative healthcare.

Vatenfall also has a branch in Poland (Vatenfall Heat Poland SA). This unit employs more than 1,100 employees (including nearly 400 individuals aged 50+). The company is also aware that, in connection with the acquisition of pension entitlements by almost 50% of the staff by 2017, steps aimed at preventing the depletion of knowledge and experience have to be taken. The necessary actions had to be taken as soon as possible because training a new employee in the energy sector takes approximately 1.5 years. By this time, they are usually working under the supervision of a colleague with extensive experience — a mentor. A yearly "Vattenfall Expert" programme was also created, addressed to high-class specialists in the energy industry, the majority of whom have already reached 50 years of age. The aim of the programme is to promote the sharing of knowledge, under the premise that "teaching others, we teach ourselves". The program was implemented in the form of workshops on knowledge management, creativity, communication, collaboration and art of self-presentation. Participants in the programme have been provided with individual coaching. This cycle was summarized by presentations of individual projects implemented within the framework of study visits. In the strategic perspective, the internal experts will play an important role in the introduction of new employees and talent management. Another internal project carried out in Vattenfall Heat Poland S.A. is the "Academy of Champion Skills". This programme is directed to the foremen of production and relates primarily to the development of competence related to knowledge, attitudes and skills. The purpose of this programme is developing leadership skills and ability to motivate and manage a team. [This information was obtained from: http://www.zysk50plus.pl/?module=Companies&action=GetCompany& companyId=144&sectionId=6, as of 14 December 2013]

6. 3. Women - an important asset of an enterprise

The low economic activity of women is a problem faced by many countries. At the same time, attention is drawn to the untapped potential that lies within this part of the population. The issues of mobilizing the potential of entrepreneurship, and the change of entrepreneurial culture are also discussed at the European level.

Good practices in the area of women's entrepreneurship have also been identified during the implementation of the QUICK IGA project. The possibility of their transfer to the southern countries of the Baltic Sea Region are presented in the prepared reports [Grzesiak, Olczyk, Starnawska 2013 and Grzesiak, Olczyk, Richert-Kaźmierska, Starnawska 2013]. Some examples of good practice are presented below. The presented descriptions are taken directly from the reports.

6. 3. 1. Pay Equity Action Plan

This practice was originally implemented in Sweden by Equal Opportunities Ombudsman (JamO). The Pay Equity Action Plan obliges enterprises to implement a specific policy concerning equal pay, i.e. to reduce the differences between salaries for the same post, for comparable work (between work in male- or female dominated jobs). The target group consisted exclusively of enterprises/organizations with more than 10 employees.

Each year, employers must prepare a plan describing their efforts to promote gender equality. The plan shall contain a survey of different measures which are required at the workplace and shall indicate which of such measures the employer intends to initiate or implement during the coming year" [http://ec.europa.eu /employment_social/equal/data/document/0801_gender_twinning_en.pdf, p.58]:

a) Working conditions: employers must take whatever steps may be required, insofar as their resources and general circumstances permit, to ensure that working conditions are suitable for both women and men.
b) Employers shall facilitate the combination of gainful employment and parenthood with respect to both female and male employees.
c) Employers shall take measures to forestall and prevent any employee from being subjected to gender-related harassment, to sexual harassment or to victimisation.
d) Recruitment, etc.: employers shall, through training, skills development and other suitable measures, promote an equal distribution between women and men in various types of work and within different categories of employees.
e) Employers shall endeavour to ensure that both women and men apply for vacant positions.
f) Employers are required to formulate a pay equity action plan in order to ensure that remuneration is fixed on the basis of objective criteria that are common to all jobs. The employer must take into account following criteria: qualifications, responsibilities, efforts and working conditions."

Each year, employers are required to carry out a pay survey and analyse their pay policies and practices, even in cases where there was no disparity identified in the previous year. Following the survey, the employer must develop a pay equity action plan which includes the results of the pay survey, an analysis of the pay system and the planned approach to identify and correct pay inequalities in the system. The plan must list: the envisaged measures to eliminate the pay differentials, an estimate of the related costs and a timeframe that cannot exceed three years. A report concerning how the planned measures have been implemented must be included in the plan for the following year.

To measure the results of introduction of Pay Equality Action Plan, number of surveys have been carried out by JamO. An initial review covers 900 pay surveys carried out between 2001 and 2005. According to JamO, pay adjustments were made for at least 100 employers, or 11% of the total. Some 1000 employees had their pay adjusted on the basis of the principle of equal pay for equal work and 160 occupational groups, involving 9000 employees, had their pay adjusted in the context of equal pay for jobs of equal value. JamO, however, draws attention to the scant reliability of data regarding the number of employees affected. In 2004–2005, an additional survey was carried out in 50 organizations (10 from the municipal sector and 40 from the private sector) that had received support from JamO. The survey revealed that the pay adjustments that were required in 24 cases were all carried out (JamO 2005). This demonstrates that, even under a compulsory legal system, support and follow-up by specialized bodies is essential in ensuring fullest enforcement by companies. It is why JamO offers consultation and advisory service in relation to the development and implementation of pay equity action plans. With a view to helping SME to meet the requirements of the Act, JamO has also materials to guide SMEs in the implementation of pay equity plans. Last survey done by JamO shows that 25% of private companies and 75% of public authorities have implemented statutory equality plans.

Due to such great efficiency of Pay Equality Action Plan in Sweden, Finland adopted quite a similar system in year 2005.

6. 3. 2. Women@Work

This practice was originally implemented in United Kingdom by Workers Educational Association. The target group were employed women who have job experience.

Initiative providing training and information for women. It gives women skill development via a learning programme, more ability to express their concerns about gender issues at workplace, in families and communities where they live, as well as to use their full potential in these environments.

This undertaking involves different bodies and industries. W@W has its own advisory group consisting of representatives from public, private and third sectors.

W@W involves employed women who have job experience and also focuses on more isolated women as a result of living in rural areas.

— It provides forum where ideas and opinions are exchanged.
— Also, it supports women to share experiences via networking thus making contacts and growing in confidence.

— It promotes women leadership via trainings and consultation on national and international level.
— It also organizes regular network meetings, speeches of guests, trainings and workshops.

6. 3. 3. Female future mobilizing talents –a business perspective

This practice was originally implemented in Norway by the Confederation of Norwegian Enterprise (NHO). The aim of the project is to bring more women into top management positions as well as into the companies' boardrooms. The target group were talented women working in private enterprises.

The NHO set up the Female Future project in 2003, and it lasted to 2008. The goals of the project were [Women in business leadership: http://www.nho.no/ff/]: to increase the percentage of women in decision-making processes, in management and in boards in general; to cause that the private sector is viewed as an attractive place to work by women; to involve managers as prime movers in the process aimed at recruiting more women to executive positions and to board posts; to make executive responsibilities be more easily combined with family responsibilities — the balance between work and private life.

First step of the programme consisted in building a network of supportive ambassadors for the project. The NHO chose influential individuals to be ambassadors, people who could address the arguments why women in business are important. What is important, these ambassadors had to be both men and women.

The second step was the selection of companies (not women!) which are interested in the project. The enterprises were recruited into the programme and the manager of the enterprise had to sign a contract. In these contracts the managers confirmed that they would work to get one, two or more women into management and into the board of directors. Also, the firms were obligated to nominate women — the candidates to Femmale Future programme — from his/her own enterprises, to pay the costs relating to participation in the Female Future programme and to facilitate a good work-life balance.

Then the management of the companies which decided to join the Female Future was asked to look for the female talents in their organisation, i.e. women who they considered to have talent and potential to take on more challenging tasks and leader positions. The selected talents joined the Female Future programme for one year and become part of the strong Female Future network.

The Female Future training programme consists of three parts: Personal leadership training, Board competence and rhetoric. The training lasted from 13 to 15 days. In addition, throughout the duration of the project, the selected women worked together with the managers of companies.

The first phase of the Female Future Programme was carried out in four rounds from the autumn of 2003 until the spring of 2005. As of spring 2006, approximately 370 talents have gone through the Phase 1 programme. More than 200 women finished the extended programme in June of 2007. In the autumn of the year 2007, 250 more women participated in the extended programme, ending at the end of 2008. In summary, since the start up in 2004 more than 1151 hand-picked talented individuals have qualified to take on board posts and more demanding leadership tasks. Approximately 700 companies have joined the programme.

First results of the programme was very optimistic: 26% of the participants in the national programme have been offered board positions during or after the Female Future Programmes (larger PLCs companies, total 490 in Norway) and 50% have been offered board positions in several regional projects following their participation in the FF Project. This was an extremely good score and promising for all the smaller limited companies which are in majority in Norway. Last evaluation of the programme was done in May 2010: 62% of the participants were offered board positions or advanced in their management career.

The Female Future programme was appointed by ILO as one of the 10 best examples on Gender Equality. Japan, Austria and Uganda are initiating a Female Future program.

6. 3. 4. Women into Technology

This practice was originally implemented in Scotland by Fife Women's Technology Centres. The aim of the project is to provide a comprehensive, fully supported training programme related to ICT sector. The target group were women (18+) with low or no previous qualifications, who have been out of the labour market for long periods.

One of the largest problems related with the low participation of women in the labour market in the BSR countries is their under-representation in higher level ICT jobs. It is especially important, as the ICT sector is characterized by significant jobs growth dynamics.

Fife Women's Technology Centres (FWTC) were established in 1990 as a positive action initiative in order to train women who experienced real difficulty in obtaining work, so that they could rejoin the work force or take up further training opportunities. Their key priority was to widen horizons and raise aspirations by offering high quality training focussing on non-traditional areas, e.i. computing, electronics and IT.

The Programme "Women into Technology" started in year1992, which was aimed first of all at long term unemployed women, at lonely parents, black and minority ethnic women, and women with disabilities. The programme was financed in 26% from European Social Fund and the rest from local and national funding.

To be able to offer to the right path for entry into the labour market, the FWTC created the network of local partners. FWTC liaised with local specialist organizations (e.g. violence against women) to ensure all round support for women, with employers (e.g. local businesses, mostly SMEs, larger manufacturing companies, banks, authorities) and with other partners specializing in an exchange of job information, in the work placement or in identification of employment opportunity. FWTC chose Adam Smith College, which accredited all courses and provided the internal verification.

WIT Core Programme covers 2,5 days per week over 48 weeks and consists of modules in maths, communication, technology and IT. The integrated part of this programme is the course of personal development, which covers to confidence building, assertiveness and team work. After this part, women could choose their professional specialization and take part in "professional progress". For example the "Office Administration" training lasts 2 days per week over 24 weeks. It includes doing European Computer Driving Licence, improvement of practical office skills and the work placement (8–12 week) with a local employer. Another example of professional progression training is "the Technical IT programme". It consists of 2 days per week training over 48 weeks in areas like Electric and Electronic Engineering, Computer Support, Network Support, Computing, Mechatronic Engineering. Additionally to the progression programmes, all women participate in a personal development programme. It covers life coaching, personal presentation, CV writing, job search application and interview skills.

All courses are free of charge and additionally FWTC covers travel and childcare costs. If possible, the expenses related to the purchase of books or exams fees are covered by Fife Women's Technology Centres. However, the key success factors of training under WIT programme is the complex and integrated approach (materials, teaching methods) which guarantees a success path to the employment. Women who took part in this project indicated a supportive atmosphere connected with a high standard as a success factor.

FWTC won the Best Practice Award in ICT and was commended for the Equal Opportunities Award at the European Social Fund Objective 3 Awards.

6. 3. 5. Fuuturi: Women entrepreneurs and managers in the future

This practice was originally implemented in Finland by Ylä-Savo Municipal Federation of Education. The target group were women entrepreneurs in existing business or women managers and employees.

North Savo is a sparsely populated area in Finland. This project was a continuation of three earlier projects of the same aim but previously focused on women start-ups.

It started with a company Futuuri ('associated with the future') owned by a woman. This initiative ran between 2008–2011 and focused on developing existing businesses owned by women. The initiative is co-financed by the ESF, the North-Savo Centre for Economic Development, Transport and the Environment (ELY), the Regional Council of North Savo, Ylä-Savon Kehitys Oy, municipalities and companies.

The project was implemented by North Savo Education, the University of Kuopio and the Savonia University of Applied Sciences.

The aims of the initiative were as follows:

— To promote women's entrepreneurship and management by speeding up the growth of enterprises and helping in the internationalization of the businesses, and also by supporting the participants' own business development projects.
— To develop the know-how and self-esteem of women entrepreneurs and managers has also been a goal. In addition, there has been a goal to develop each enterprise's knowledge-intensive service and product innovations.
— To support co-operation in networks among women.
Activities of the project included: a course with teaching methods like lectures, discussions, and study trips (excursions) built around seven separate modules (business management, implementation of a change in an enterprise, doing business electronically, internationalization, economic control of an enterprise, legal knowledge, marketing and communication). The same courses were held in 3 different locations for their benefit. The women also participated in volunteer-based development circles where they could exchange ideas — they also had opportunity to gain support from other women working in the same sector of the economy. They could benefit from

coaching. A fee of 500 Euros for three years was included. These activities were held during one meeting per week – sometimes in the evenings and sometimes at weekends.

6. 4. A new dimension of education

6.4.1. Building a competitive advantage based on knowledge and skills

While building their competitiveness, the enterprises should reach the not fully untapped potential that lies in human resources. In this regard, the solutions used in other countries can be used (the possibilities and examples of good practice to use were covered by the author in previous chapters).

Particular attention is paid to education which not only promotes entrepreneurial attitudes but also allows for acquiring relevant business skills. The objective set out in the Europe 2020 Strategy in the field of education is [Communication from the European Commission in 2010]:

— reduction of the rate of early school leaving below 10%;
— completion of the third cycle of education (tertiary-level of education) for at least 40% of people aged 30–34 years.

In the past, various types of programmes and initiatives aimed at increasing the level of education of societies or adapting skills to labour market needs were implemented in European countries. In 2006, the European Parliament and the European Council issued a Recommendation on key competences. These include [European Union 2006, p 13]:

"1) Communication in the mother tongue;
2) Communication in foreign languages;
3) Mathematical competence and basic competences in science and technology;
4) Digital competence;
5) Learning to learn;
6) Social and civic competences;
7) Sense of initiative and entrepreneurship; and
8) Cultural awareness and expression."

Such a long-term project for increasing mobility and raising skills was also the *Lifelong Learning Programme* (Implemented in the years 2007-2013), creating possibilities and opportunities for different target groups through four sub-programmes [see: http://ec.europa.eu/education/lifelong-learning-programme/doc78_en.htm]:

— Comenius for schools;
— Erasmus for higher education;
— Leonardo da Vinci for vocational education and training;
— Grundtvig for adult education.

On the one hand, these programmes were designed to allow individuals of all ages to supplement education, on the other — they helped to develop the education sector in Europe. They were directed not only to the pupils or students, but also to the teachers who have gained new experiences e.g. through study visits.

The mid-term report [European Commission 2011 COM 413, p. 4–7, 10–11] assessed the effects of the LLP programme — first of all, it confirmed that the activities conducted within the framework of the programme were justified; however, it also identified areas requiring adjustments (for example, simplification of rules of control) or paying more attention (e.g. clarifying how the programme can contribute to achieving the objectives of the Europe 2020 Strategy). Benefits of the *Lifelong Learning Programme* implementation include the increase in the value added in three areas: strategic cooperation and exchange between the countries participating in the programme, the support of the European dimension of education and training (e.g. cooperation between educational organizations, changing structures and practices of educational institutions, the creation of mobility programs) and complementing existing international, national or bilateral programmes. The data collected during the programme indicate progress in the implementation of quantitative targets. Over 60% of the budgeted funds of the project were allocated to support the transnational mobility. The largest share of the funds was allocated to students going on exchange under the Erasmus programme. The employability and entrepreneurship of participants were greatly influenced by the internships constituting a part of the *Leonardo da Vinci* programme. These activities also involved SMEs, which have employed about 80% of all trainees. In turn, due to the employee participation in the *Grundtvig non-vocational adult education programme* an increase in mobility was observed also in this group. The *Comenius* programme enabled the implementation of measures aimed at improving the quality of education — on both the primary and the secondary level — by increasing the mobility of teachers and students.

The Communication of the European Commission [European Commission 2012 COM 669] highlighted the importance of investing in education and training to enhance growth and competitiveness. Higher qualifications mean more possibilities of increasing productivity and in the long-term perspective can stimulate growth and innovation, as well as shape the future labour market. It was also found that European education and training systems are still inadequate to ensure the skills that increase employment opportunities. The educational institutions occasionally establish cooperation with enterprises or employers to make the learning process closer to economic reality. It was emphasized that currently one of the main problems in the labour market is how it mismatches the requirements of the labour market [see also: European Commission 2012 COM 582]. The document highlights the increase in the percentage of college and university graduates, but still emphasizes the need to take action to achieve the goal of achieving a college or university education by 40% of young people. The proportion of early school leavers is still too high. Thus, the basic tasks faced by the education systems in different countries relate primarily to enabling the acquisition of employability-increasing competences. Recommendations for the European countries have been developed in separate documents [see summaries: http://ec.europa.eu/europe2020/index_pl.htm].

The use of open technologies in education and training provides opportunities to increase not only economic growth but also indicators of innovativeness, productivity and employment. It also allows for the acquisition of new skills needed in a changing labour market. Implementing the European Union's policy in this area is to be supported by the Erasmus and Horizon 2020 programmes, the structural funds or the Open Method of Coordination in Education and Training in 2020. The opportunities should be used by all the Member States and regions, however especially by those less developed. When updating the strategic documents, attention needs to be paid to changes in the system. It frequently happens that regulations concerning curricula and the assessment of practices make it difficult to take full advantage of the potential of open technologies. In university education changes are also inhibited by other factors — these are usually budgetary constraints and inflexible management structure. High potential of introduction of ICT structural changes in adult education is also created by the possibility to reduce the cost of training and increase the flexibility of access (time and place) [see also: [European Commission 654, p. 3–4]

It is emphasized that by 2020, 20% more jobs will require higher qualifications. Satisfying this demand requires teaching young people entrepreneurship and skills to adapt to the inevitable changes in the labour market during their entire careers. This in turn implies the need to raise standards and implement changes in education systems.

6.4.2. Financing adult education

Lifelong learning is part of the concept of learning throughout life for individuals who have completed formal education. The documents of the European Commission list the activities related to lifelong learning which should be carried out in countries, such as the development and modernization of adult education, the development of guidance services utilizing the possibilities of ICT, identification of factors motivating people to pursue education, as well as promoting and developing new approaches to learning. As a result, the Council of the European Union's considered the strategic objectives to be: [European Commission 2009, p. 1192]

— implementation of the concept of lifelong learning and mobility,
— improving the quality and efficiency of education and training,
— promoting equity, social cohesion and active citizenship and
— enhancing creativity and innovativeness, including entrepreneurship, at all levels of education and training.

The achievement of these objectives, as well as the objectives set out in the Europe 2020 strategy, requires incurring adequate expenses to enable the implementation of policy guidelines. A downward trend rate of expenditure on the implementation of labour market policies in by far most countries of the Baltic Sea Region in relation to GDP can be observed in the period 2003–2011. It is true, however, that in many countries there has been an increase in the proportion of GDP spent on activities related to the labour market after 2007 but in 2011 the indicator declined again. Only in Denmark it was higher than in the previous year (see Table.53).

Table 53. Public expenditures on labour market policy (% GDP) in 2003–2011

Country	2003	2004	2005	2006	2007	2008	2009	2010	2011
EU28	-	-	2.00	1.82	1.60	1.61	2.17	-	-
DK	4.39	4.34	3.77	3.23	2.66	2.41	3.20	3.65	3.73
DE	3.48	3.42	3.00	2.61	2.03	1.91	2.53	2.27	1.81
EE	0.26	0.23	0.19	0.15	0.15	0.28	1.60	1.10	0.72
LV	0.49	0.51	0.54	0.55	0.46	0.48	1.34	1.24	0.69
LT	0.35	0.30	0.34	0.39	0.41	0.39	0.91	0.79	0.56
PL	-	-	1.28	1.16	1.01	0.91	0.96	1.04	0.72
FI	2.93	2.96	2.77	2.57	2.26	2.13	2.75	2.79	2.46
SE	2.36	2.44	2.40	2.25	1.71	1.39	1.79	1.86	1.69
NO	1.66	1.61	1.58	1.07	0.96	-	-	-	-

Source: own based on Eurostat data http://appsso.eurostat.ec.europa.eu/nui/show.do? dataset=lmp_ind_exp&lang=en (12.11.2013).

In contrast, in the period 2000–2009 public expenditure (expressed in relation to GDP) on education and training only in Denmark, Finland, Sweden and Norway was higher than the European average (EU = 27) (see Table 54). It does not bode well to the achievement of the targets defined in the Europe 2020 strategy.

Table 54. Total public expenditures on education and training (% GDP) in 2000–2010

Country/ Year	2001	2002	2003	2004	2005	2006	2007	2008	2009	2010
EU27	5.02	5.12	5.17	5.09	5.06	5.06	4.97	5.09	5.44	5.48
DK	8.44	8.44	8.33	8.43	8.30	7.97	7.81	7.68	8.74	8.80
EE	5.24	5.47	5.29	4.92	4.88	4.70	4.72	5.59	6.09	5.68
FI	6.06	6.22	6.43	6.42	6.30	6.18	5.90	6.10	6.81	6.84
DE	4.51	4.72	4.74	4.62	4.57	4.43	4.49	4.57	5.06	5.08
LV	5.71	5.77	5.34	5.08	5.09	5.09	5.02	5.75	5.64	5.01
LT	5.86	5.81	5.14	5.17	4.88	4.82	4.64	4.87	5.64	5.38
NO	7.18	7.58	7.55	7.42	6.97	6.49	6.66	6.40	7.24	6.87
PL	5.42	5.41	5.35	5.41	5.47	5.25	4.91	5.08	5.09	5.17
SE	7.06	7.36	7.21	7.09	6.89	6.75	6.61	6.76	7.26	6.98

Source: own based on Eurostat data http://epp.eurostat.ec.europa.eu/portal/page/portal/ education/data/database (16.12.2013).

On the other hand, while analysing the percentage of people aged 24–64 years participating in lifelong learning in the period 2006–2012, it can be seen that in the Nordic countries, where learning is a lifelong has a long tradition, it is significantly higher than in other countries in the Baltic Sea Region and the EU average (EU = 27).

Table 55. Percentage of the adult population aged 25 to 64 participating in education and training in 2006–2012 (M – male, F – female)

Country	2006		2007		2008		2009		2010		2011		2012	
	M	F	M	F	M	F	M	F	M	F	M	F	M	F
EU27	8.6	10.4	8.4	10.2	8.5	10.2	8.4	10.2	8.3	10	8.2	9.6	8.4	9.7
DK	24.6	33.8	23.8	34.3	24.8	35.2	25.3	37.2	26	39.1	25.6	39	25.4	37.8
EE	4.2	8.6	4.6	9.3	6.6	12.6	7.6	13.2	8.6	13	9.2	14.5	10.6	14.9
FI	19.3	27	19.4	27.5	19.3	26.9	18.5	25.9	18.9	27.1	19.9	27.7	20.7	28.4
DE	7.7	7.2	8	7.6	8	7.8	7.8	7.7	7.7	7.6	7.9	7.7	8	7.8
LV	4.1	9.3	4.6	9.3	4.3	9	3.6	6.9	3.4	6.5	3.8	6.2	6	7.9
LT	2.9	6.6	3.6	6.8	3.7	6.1	3.6	5.4	3.2	4.8	4.4	6.9	4.3	5.9
NO	17.2	20.2	17.1	18.9	18.2	20.5	16.8	19.5	16.4	19.2	17.1	19.2	18.8	21.3
PL	4.3	5.1	4.7	5.5	4.2	5.2	4.3	5.1	4.8	5.9	4	5	3.8	5.1
SE	13.3	23.7	13.1	24.3	16.1	28.4	16.1	28.5	18	30.9	18.5	31.6	20	33.5

Source: own based on Eurostat data
http://epp.eurostat.ec.europa.eu/portal/page/portal/education/data/database (16.12.2013).

6.4.3. Forecasting demand for qualifications [36]

---

[36] The problem of forecasting the demand for skills has also been discussed in [Grzesiak 2012].

Due to the need to improve labour mobility in Europe, boost skills and eliminate the mismatch between skills and labour market needs, forecasting skills is a necessary measure. This mismatch of skills, or even the lack of employees with particular skills, is already visible in some sectors. Forecasts related to changes in the sectors will certainly have an impact also on the demand for specific qualifications. It can also be expected that due to changes in the ways of working a kind of polarization of demand for skills will emerge. An increase in demand both for highly skilled professionals and for workers with additional skills, employed in sales and distribution, is predicted [Cedefop 2009, p. 15–21] (see also Figure 34).

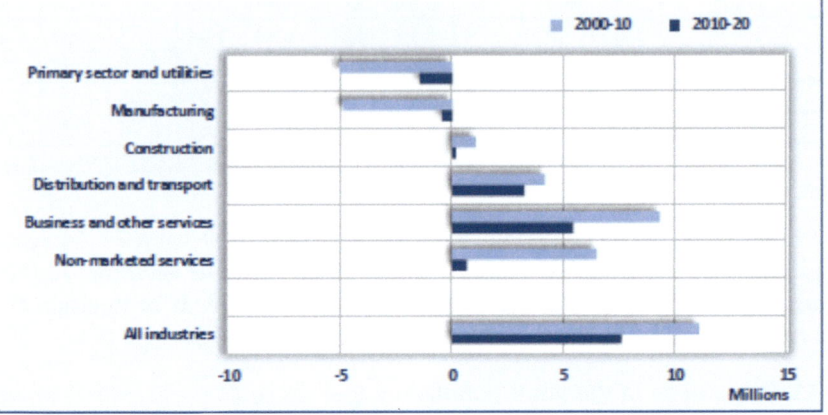

Figure 34. Past and likely future sectoral employment change, 2000–10 and 2010–20 EU27+
Source: [Cedefop… Forecast 2012].

As has been mentioned in Chapter 4, one of the challenges faced by Europe is the ageing of population. Statistical data show that in 2030, almost 24% of the population will be of retirement age, and in the year 2060 this percentage will increase to almost 30%. In some countries (such as Poland, Germany, Latvia, Lithuania and Estonia) the number of individuals aged over 65 years will exceed the European average. This will have consequences for employers, who will have to rely on the skills and experience of older workers. Delay of leaving the labour market seems inevitable, also because of the need to maintain balance in the pension systems and — in general — social security. The social policy should aim at maintaining good overall health and determining the optimal retirement age. Increased migration within the European Union and the influx of foreign labour[37] can also be expected.

Forecasting skills requires a number of tasks — both in the short-term and medium- and long term perspective. It is proposed [Cedefop 2009, p. 69–75] to develop in the short term a model of supply and demand for qualifications, which will require the involvement of national experts. However, in the medium term a correction of the model will be needed and the search for alternative tools to measure qualification mismatches and improving the quality of data at European level. The report [Cedefop 2013] presents the results of pilot studies conducted in nine European countries (including Finland, Poland and Germany) to determine the qualifications expected by employers in various sectors. The summary of the characteristics of the two approaches used in the study is presented in the following table.

Table 56. Summary of characteristics of the two alternative proposals

	Sector-based survey	Generic skills survey
Key features added-value	— enables quantitative case studies of selected occupations in sectors of key interests — detailed insights into changing skill needs — covers generic skills	— representative of entire EU economy and broad occupational groups — looks at generic skills and newly-emerging tasks — Measures drivers of change in skill needs and provides an EU-wide overview of their impact
Drawbacks	— does not cover the whole EU economy but a small subset of priority occupations in sectors — - broad-brush comparisons between countries are not feasible across a range of occupations	— no detailed information on sectoral trends — omits occupation-specific tasks — does not provide detailed information on individual occupations (at ISCO-08 3 or 4 digits)
Next steps	— choice of sectors and occupations — improve comparability of importance scale; streamline coding of newly-emerging tasks — develop task lists, pre-test	— focus the survey instruments on generic skills — improve comparability of importance scale; streamline coding newly-emerging tasks — pre-test finalised instruments

---

[37] The issues of demographic change in Europe and changes in demand for different qualifications are also shown in [Cedefop, 2010].

	final instruments	

Source: [Cedefop 2013].

However, in the long term the needs of employers should also be studied, a common European approach to development should be elaborated and the confrontation of the results with the model should be made in with a view to identification of any discrepancies. Allocation of certain funds for the implementation of these tasks at the regional, national and European level is also important.

During the implementation of various studies [e.g. Cedefop 2009] it was noted that in some sectors a European labour market has already been established, whereas some others have undergone significant restructuring while adapting to the requirements of the knowledge-based economy. The observed trends will affect the future demand for specific qualifications. Satisfying this demand, particularly in the area of new technologies and innovations, is necessary for increasing the competitiveness of the European Union.

References

1. Bogan C.E., English M.J. (1994), *Benchmarking for Best Practices: Winning Through Innovative Adaptation*, New York: McGraw-Hill.
2. EFILWC–European Foundation for the Improvement of Living and Working Conditions (1997), *Combating Age Barriers in Employment. Research Summary*, Dublin.
3. European Commission (2011), Report from the Commission to The European Parliament, The Council and Social Committee and the Committee of the Regions, *Mid term review of the Lifelong Learning Programme*, COM(2011) 413 final, Brussels.
4. European Commission (2012), Communication from the Commision to The European Parliament, The Council and Social Committee and the Committee of the Regions *Rethinking Education: Investing in skills for better socio-economics outcomes*, COM(2012) 669 final, Starsburg.
5. European Commission (2013), Commission Staff working Document, *Analysis and mapping of innovative teaching and learning Technologies and Open Educational Resources in Europe*, SWD(2013) 341 final, BrusselsEurolink Age (2000), Ageing in Employment A proposal for a European Code of Good Practice, Eurolink Age, London.
6. European Commission (2013), Communication from the Commision to The European Parliament, The Council and Social Committee and the Committee of the Regions, *Opening up Education: Innovative teaching and learning for all through new Technologies and OpenEducational Resources*, COM(2013) 654 final, Brussels.
7. European Union (2006), *Recommendation of the European Parliamnet and of the Council on the key competences for lifelong learning*, Official Journal of the European Union L 394, 30.12.2006 p. 10-18, Brussels, (2006/962/EC).
8. European Union, Council notices from European Union institutions and bodies (2009), *Council conclusions on a strategic framework for European cooperation in education and training ("ET 2020")*, Official Journal of the European Union C 119/2 (2009/C 119/02), part IV, 28.05.2009.
9. *Future Skills Supply and Demand in Europe: Forecast* (2012), Cedefop, European Centre for the Development of Vocational Training, Luxembourg.
10. Grzesiak M., *Kształcenie ustawiczne – trendy w krajach regionu Morza Bałtyckiego* [in] Richert-Kaźmierska A. (ed.) *Przedsiębiorstwo we współczesnej gospodarce - teoria i praktyka*, No 3 2012, pp. 5-16.
11. Grzesiak M., Olczyk M., Richert-Kaźmierska A., Starnawska M. (2013), *The best practices transfer part II*, Report produced within Work Package 4 of the EU-funded project QUICK IGA.
12. Grzesiak M., Olczyk M., Starnawska M. (2013), *The best practices transfer part I*, Report produced within Work Package 4 of the EU-funded project QUICK IGA.

13. Grzesiak M., Richert-Kaźmierska A. (2013), *The analysis of the conditions for best practices' transfer*, Report produced within Work Package 4 of the EU-funded project QUICK IGA.

14. Harper K. (1996), *Benchmarking: International Clearinghouse Plays Matchmaker for Companies That Want to Improve*, Arkansas Business, vol.9, (1996).

15. Kuczewska J. (2007), *Europejska procedura benchmarkingu. Programy i działania*, Polska Agencja Rozwoju przedsiębiorczości, Warszawa.

16. Naegele G., Walker A. (2006), *A guide to good practice in age management*, European Foundation for the Improvement of Living and Working Conditions.

17. OECD (2011), *Tertiary Education for the Knowledge Society*. Pointers for the policy development, OECD Publishing.

18. *Skills for Europe's future: Anticipating Occupational Skill Needs* (2009), Cedefop, European Centre for the Development of Vocational Training, Luxembourg.

19. *Skills Supply and Demand in Europe: Medium-Term Forecast up to 2020* (2010), Cedefop, European Centre for the Development of Vocational Training, Luxembourg.

20. *Skills Supply and Demand in Europe: Methodological framework* (2012), Cedefop, European Centre for the Development of Vocational Training, Luxembourg.

21. Taylor P. (2006), *Employment initiatives for an ageing workforce in the EU15*, European Foundation for the Improvement of Living and Working Conditions, Dublin.

22. Walker A., Taylor P. (1998), *Combating Age Barriers in Employment. A European Portfolio of Good Practice*, European Foundation for the Improvement of Living and Working Conditions, Dublin.

23. Communication from the European Commission (2010), *Europe 2020 - A strategy for smart, sustainable and inclusive growth*, COM (2010) 2020 final version, Brussels 3.3.2010

Publications of the Baltic Sea Academy

Volume 1
Strategies for the Development of Crafts and SMEs
in the Baltic Sea Region
2011
ISBN: 9783842326125

Volume 2
Strategy Programme for education policies in the Baltic Sea Region
2012 (2nd edition)
ISBN: 9783848252534

Volume 3
Education Policy Strategies today and tomorrow around the "Mare Balticum"
2011
IBSN: 9783842374218

Volume 4
Energy Efficiency and Climate Protection around the
Mare Balticum
2011
ISBN: 9783844800982

Volume 5
SME relevant sectors in the BSR: Personnel organisation, Energy and Construction
2012
ISBN: 9783848202577

Volume 6
Strategies and Promotion of Innovation in Regional Policies around the Mare Balticum
2012
IBSN 9783848218295

Volume 7
Strategy Programme for innovation in regional policies in the Baltic Sea Region

2012
ISBN: 9783848230471

Volume 8
Humanivity - Innovative economic development through human growth by Kenneth Daun
2012
ISBN: 9783848253395

Volume 9
Economic Perspectives, Qualification and Labour Market Integration of Women in the Baltic Sea Region
2013
ISBN: 9783732243952

Volume 10
Corporate Social Responsebility and Women's Entrepreneurship around the Mare Balticum
2013
ISBN: 9783732278459

Volume 11
Development of the enterprises' competitiveness in the context of demographic challenges
2013
ISBN: 973732293971

Volume 12
Age, Gender and Innovation –

Strategy program and action plans for the Baltic Sea Region
2014
ISBN: 9783735784919

Volume 13
Innovative SMEs by Gender and Age around the Mare Balticum
2014
ISBN: 9783735791191

Volume 14
Innovation in SMEs, previous projects in the Baltic Sea Region and future needs
2014
ISBN: 9783735791191

Volume 15
Building the socially responsible employment policy in the Baltic Sea Region
2014
ISBN: 9783735790484

Volume 16
Women and elderly on the BSR labour market - good practices' analysis and transfer
2014
ISBN: 9783735791412

Volume 17
Manual and Best Practices for Innovative SMEs by Gender and Age in the Baltic Sea Region
2014
ISBN: 9783735791405

Volume 18
Civilizational changes and the competitiveness of modern enterprises
2014
ISBN: 9783732282449

Members of the Hanse-Parlament

The Chamber of Craftmanship and Enterprise in Białystok
Brest Department of the Belarusian Chamber of Commerce and Industry
Hungarian Association of Craftsmen Corporations
Företagarna Kalmar länCottbus Chamber of Skilled Crafts and SME's
Dresden Chamber of Skilled Crafts and Small Businesses
Pomeranian Chamber of Handicrafts for SME's
Hamburg Chamber of Skilled Crafts and Small Businesses
The Federation of Finnish Enterprises
Chamber of Craft Region Kaliningrad
Kaliningrad Regional Economic Development Agency
Chamber of Crafts and SME in Katowice
Chamber of Crafts and SME in Kielce
Handicraft Chamber of Ukraine
Handicraft Chamber Leningrad Region
The Craft Chamber of Łódź
Företagarna Skåne Service AB
Belarusian Chamber of Commerce and Industry
Minsk Department of the Belarussian Chamber of Commerce and Industry
Mogilev Branch of Belarusian Chamber of Commerce and Industry
Russian Chamber of Crafts
Warmia and Mazury Chamber of Crafts and Small Business in Olsztyn
Chamber of Crafts in Opole
The Norwegian Federation of Craft Enterprises
Master of Crafts Norway
Eastern Mecklenburg-Western Pomerania Chamber of Handicraft
Panevėžys Chamber of Commerce, Industry and Crafts
Satakunnan Yrittäjät R.Y.
Wielkopolska Craft Chamber in Poznań
Latvian Chamber of Crafts
Craft Chamber in Rzeszów
Schwerin Chamber of Skilled Crafts
The Chamber of Handicraft Middle Pomerania in Słupsk
The St. Petersburg Crafts Chamber
The Chamber of Crafts and SME in Szczecin
Estonian Association of Small and Medium Enterprises
The Baltic Institute of Finland
The Organisation of Handicraft Businesses in Trondheim
Vilnius Chamber of Commerce, Industry and Crafts
Lithuanian Business Employers Confederation

The Chamber of Crafts of Mazovia, Kurpie and Podlasie Regions in Warsaw
Small Business Chamber Warsaw
The Lower Silesian Chamber of Craft and Small and Medium-sized Businesses
Kyiv Chamber of Commerce and Industry
IBC Innovationsfabrikken Kolding
Donskaya Craft Chamber in Rostov/Don
Nordic Forum of Crafts

Members of the Baltic Sea Academy

Brest State Technical University, Belarus
University 21 non-profit limited Liability Company, Germany
Hamburg University of Corporate Education, Germany
Hamburg Institute of International Economics, Germany
Hanse-Parlament e.V., Germany
International Business Academy, Denmark
Lund University, Sweden
Satakunta University of Applied Sciences, Finland
University of Latvia, Latvia
Gdansk University of Technology, Poland
Panevėžys College
Hanseatic Academy of Management, Słupsk, Poland
Saint-Petersburg State University of Economics, Russia
Tampere University of Technology, Finland
Vilnius Gediminas Technical University, Lithuania
Vilnius Pedagogical University, Lithuania
University of Bialystok, Poland
Võru County Vacational Training Centre, Estonia